Dear Debb

I pray
is such a bles
you! May God up
encourage you, &
you,
deliver you
as
Him!
you draw closer to
I will be praying
for you :)
Love,
Andrea

Daily Professions

ANDREA JOHNSON

VOL.2

Daily Profession

TRANSFORM YOUR LIFE

Daily Professions

Acknowledgments

I would like to first thank God the Father, God the Son, and God the Holy Ghost for all that He has done for me! To experience the power of God in all three forms is life transforming and fulfilling beyond what I could ever imagine; and for that, I am grateful.

To my husband, Pastor Lance T. Johnson Sr., who loves me beyond my wildest dreams, thank you for always driving me to fulfill my destiny and for being my covering and my best friend through it all.

To my children, Christian and LJ, Mom loves you so much, and there is nobody like you all! Your confidence in who you are, even at a young age, inspires me! Thank you for your encouragement, support, and always cheering me on in all my endeavors.

To my family and friends who are so much part of my foundation in Christ and who constantly help strengthen me with words of life and wisdom, I love you all to life!

Blessings abundantly to The R.O.C. Church Family, and to mentors and colleagues who have helped me to always strive to reach this next level! I am eternally grateful for each and every one of you!

Contents

Foreword

Every once and while, a book comes around that makes sense and shares the mysteries of the Kingdom of God. *Daily Professions* does just this with its insightful devotions and meaningful declarations. In a world where people of all faiths understand the need to confess their sins before God, *Daily Professions* by Andrea Johnson takes us another step from confession to profession. In this book, we are refreshed again on how important it is for us to profess every day and not just confess our sins every day. We learn to profess daily the promises of God for our lives after confessing our sins before God. This book takes you truly from a valley experience to the mountaintop experience in just one profession that can catapult you from a day of defeat to a day of triumph. When most devotions are just for reading, *Daily Professions* incorporates reading and writing so that you can get your dreams out of your head and onto paper. Soon you realize that you are writing a vision for your life; each day, you have devotion with *Daily Professions.*

When reading, writing, and meditating with *Daily Professions*, one can't help but be encouraged to be a better person and believer because it, in a nutshell, is transformative. This devotional is one that can be used personally or in a group setting that will rejuvenate each person or group to go after the things of God for their lives! This fifty-two-week devotional will keep you inspired through this next year of your life, and all shall bear witness of the transformation happening in your life right before their eyes.

It is with honor that I can introduce you to not just an incredible devotional but an incredible author, Andrea Johnson. She writes her devotionals as if she is sitting in front of you on her back porch as you both experience God in ways that you have never experienced before. Get ready to meet God all over again, and you will no longer be the caterpillar inching around the tree but will transform into the butterfly that is ready to soar to new heights in God! Enjoy!

—Pastor Lance T. Johnson Sr.
Author of *Don't Die a Caterpillar: The Power of Transformation*

Introduction

There is truly *power* in the *profession* of God's Word! We live every day of our lives with our dreams, our goals, our wants, and our desires, but we sometimes fail to draw upon the Word that He has given us to transform us so we can fulfill our purpose! This second volume of *Daily Professions* is designed to bring the deliverance we need from past issues or current situations, one day, one Bible verse at a time. It was written so that every week you can read *one* devotion you are drawn to, profess God's word on that topic, and bring about the transformation in your life that only He can give. For the reality is that Satan and his demonic forces will always try to get you off course, but like Jesus showed us in Matthew 4:10, it is the declaration of God's written word that will make you victorious over the enemy and remind you that God can continue to increase you, and move you forward through it all!

Hebrews 10:23 says, *"Let us hold fast the profession of our faith without wavering; for he is faithful that promised."* So, to help you stand firm, you will have the opportunity to read *one* devotion at the beginning of the week, with topical scriptures to declare the rest of the week that will help you *profess your faith* and live it out each day so that you can see

His promises come to pass in your life. Some of these topical scriptures have been published in my blog, but they have been presented here as well to empower your profession of God's Word and further increase your transformation.

Then, there is a *Daily Challenge* just for you that will help you put your faith into action during the week. Most importantly, it will help you do what God ultimately created you to do, which is draw closer to Him, hear His voice, and cherish your relationship with Him above anything else by writing down what He has spoken to you. If you truly believe what God has said, profess His word and journal what you have received. At the end of the week, you will be able to record how the daily profession of the Word of God has transformed your life personally in your relationship with Him, with your family and friends, in your career, and beyond!

So, go forth! Draw closer to Him every day, each week, and fall in love with the very One who loved you first (1 John 4:19). Daily profess His word for *fifty-two weeks* and expect to see God manifest His promises in your life like never before when you commit your heart, mind, body, and soul to Him. Step-by-step, day by day, He will overflow you with His presence and His power to overcome every obstacle, so you can live out your destiny with Him!

Give God one year, and God will transform your life into what He made you to be! For remember, when your destiny collides with your profession, your purpose is birthed. Your dreams that He has given you will come true so that He can get all the glory and more souls can be saved through Jesus Christ!

A Brand-New Day to Fulfill Your Destiny!

This is a brand-new day, and there is so much that God has in store for you, but are you willing to go get it? He knows the plans He has for you. Like the sun at sunset, when the orange and reddish rays shoot across the expanse of the sky, He reminds us that He is the Creator of heaven and earth, and there is no limit to what He can do! However, are you making strides to go after Him and fulfill His plan for your life? We must be willing to ask ourselves, Are we living the life God has ordained to the utmost, or are we stuck in a rut on neutral? Are we accomplishing our goals for this year, or are we consumed with something that happened last month or earlier in the year that we can't seem to get over? This day, like any other day, has a brand-new, clean slate for you to achieve your goals, experience something new in Christ, and have the joy that only He can give. We just have to seek His direction to receive it. God tells us intimately in Psalm 32:8 that *"I will instruct you and teach thee in the way which thou shalt go; I will fix mine eyes upon thee."* He has you and will lovingly guide you to experience a life you have never dreamed of. Just follow Him and do what He tells you to do. Your destiny in Him awaits…go after Him and get it!

Daily Profess God's Word for *a Brand New Day*

I will instruct you and teach thee in the way which thou shalt go; I will fix mine eyes upon thee. (Ps. 32:8)

For the vision [is] yet for an appointed time, but at the end it shall speak, and not lie: though it tarry, wait for it; because it will surely come, it will not tarry. (Hab. 2:3)

So shall my word be that goeth forth out of my mouth: it shall not return unto me void, but it shall accomplish that which I please, and it shall prosper [in the thing] whereto I sent it. (Is 55:11

I the Lord search the heart, [I] try the reins, even to give every man according to his ways, [and] according to the fruit of his doings. (Jer. 17:10)

And we know that all things work together for good to them that love God, to them who are the called according to [his] purpose. (Rom. 8:28)

Commit thy works unto the LORD, and thy thoughts shall be established. (Prov. 16:3)

Hear counsel, and receive instruction, that thou mayest be wise in thy latter end. (Prov. 19:20)

For I know the thoughts that I think toward you, saith the LORD, thoughts of peace, and not of evil, to give you an expected end. (Jer. 29:11)

There are many plans in a man's heart; nevertheless, the counsel of the LORD, that shall stand. (Prov. 19:21)

And your ears shall hear a word behind you, saying, This is the way, walk you in it, when you turn to the right hand, and when you turn to the left. (Is. 30:21)

Which scripture speaks to you the most and why?

____

____

____

____

____

____

____

____

A Daily Challenge for You

This profession should jump-start you like never before! Whatever God is calling you to do, I want to encourage you to make some type of step or stride toward it this week. Whatever you have to do, take the time to pray first and determine what you can do this week that will move you closer to your destiny. It may be making a phone call, picking up a pen to write a book, outlining a plan of action, or talking to someone in your field of interest. Whatever it is, make sure to follow God's lead and let nothing stop you from accomplishing it. He is waiting on you!

In pursuit of my destiny, this week I will...

This, I profess in Jesus' name!

Daily Profession of the Word of God Transformed My Life This Week by...

A New Level

There is something about being on a new level in your life; a place you have never been before. You look at your surroundings and you just take them in. It is like seeing the ocean for the first time, or gazing at the gorgeous set of mountains and the open terrain. You are so excited to be here, in awe of its beauty, and you anticipate what happiness it can bring.

Being on a new level in your walk with Christ, on a new level in your career, or even just having a new mind-set, can make you look at things differently. It will cause you to pray and draw closer to God more as you check out the lay of the land and examine the people therein. However, you can also be overwhelmed by this new environment and even feel lonely in this unfamiliar place. Anybody will tell you that gazing at the ocean and the mountains is amazing, but if you go in the ocean and go up into the mountains, you begin to see the dangers therein. You slowly start learning what to do and what not to do, how to succeed, how to survive, and how to live.

This is why the most important thing you can do on this new level is seek God's face! Colossians 3:10 says, *"I have put on the new self and I am being renewed to a true knowledge according to the image of the One who created me."* Ask Him every morning for direction, and ask Him to teach you through His Word so that you can stand upon it as you learn this new terrain that God has brought you into. For it can be joyous and exciting, but it can also become overwhelming and consume you if you don't grow in the wisdom God has given you for the new level you are in! So, enjoy it, rejoice in what God has done, and prepare to go to heights unknown, experiencing all that God has for you. Just don't forget to stay humble, seek Him first, and let Him lead the way.

Daily Profess God's Word for "*A New Level*"

I have put on the new self and I am being renewed to a true knowledge according to the image of the One who created me. (Col. 3:10)

I have been buried with Christ by baptism of death and raised up by the glory of God, and I am walking in the newness of life God has given me. (Rom. 6:4)

Because I am in Christ I am a new creature! Old things are passed away and behold, all things are become new. (2 Cor. 5:17)

The God of all grace, who has called me to His eternal glory by Christ Jesus, after I have suffered a while, will make me perfect, establish, strengthen, and settle me. (1 Pet. 5:10)

I am renewed in the spirit of my mind, and I put on the new man, which after God has been created in righteousness and true holiness. (Eph. 4:23-24)

A new commandment He has given to me is to love one another, even as He has loved me. By this men will know that I am His disciple if I have love one for another. (Jn 13:34-35)

A new commandment has been given to me, which is true in Him, because the darkness is past and the true light now shines. (1 John 2:7-8)

Behold, God is doing a new thing in me, and now it will spring forth; shall I not know it? He will make a way in the wilderness and rivers in the desert. (Is 43:19)

Behold God will make all things new. These words are true and faithful. (Rev. 21:5)

Which scripture speaks to you the most and why?

____

____

____

____

____

____

____

____

____

A Daily Challenge for You

You have entered a new season in your life, and God wants you to enjoy it, embrace Him, and learn this new territory that you are in. So make sure to take the necessary steps each day to spend time with Him and find out what His will for your life is. As you check out the new terrain and get acclimated, remember that God is the one who brought you into this new place. He is the One who will guide you through and establish you.

On this new level, God is telling me to…

This, I profess in Jesus' name!

Daily Profession of the Word of God Transformed My Life This Week By…

A Passion for Christ

It is an amazing thing when you finally get to the point that you want to accomplish what God has set before you and nothing is going to stop you. During my time of prayer and fasting this year, I realized that God is calling us higher in Him. He is calling for the body of Christ to exercise the gifts He has given us and move in what He has called us to do for His glory!

We can get so caught up in man and what people do or with circumstances that are going on in our lives, and it can simmer down our passion to do what we do for Christ. However, one thing my momma always used to say to me is, "This, too, shall pass." In other words, you can't get stuck here. We should be more focused on receiving the fresh daily bread, the daily Word that God wants to give us so we can fulfill our destiny and reach more souls for Him. Time does go by fast, and we don't know the day or the hour, so we have to seek God's face for wisdom and direction and do what He says to do. Deuteronomy 4:29 says, *"But from there you will seek the Lord your God, and you will find Him if you seek Him with all your heart and with all your soul."* God is waiting to pour out His spirit upon you and move you in your purpose. He is waiting this year to give you everything you need to advance in your destiny.

All you need to do is place your expectation in Him. Your confidence comes from Him! Your peace comes from Him! Your passion and drive to do what God is calling you to do comes from God, and there is nothing Satan can do to stop what He has ordained. The only person who can stop it is you. So, declare that today is a new day, and I will live in my passion for Christ, fulfill my destiny, and be a witness for Christ!

Daily Profess God's Word for *"A Passion for Christ"*

But from there you will seek the Lord your God, and you will find Him if you seek Him with all your heart and with all your soul. (Deut. 4:29)

So shall the knowledge of wisdom be to your soul; If you have found it, there is a prospect, and your hope will not be cut off. (Prov. 24:14)

I know the thoughts that I think toward you, saith the Lord, thoughts of peace, and not of evil, to give you an expected end. (Jer. 29:11)

For surely there is an end; and thine expectation shall not be cut off. (Prov. 23:18)

According to my earnest expectation and hope that in nothing I shall be ashamed, but with all boldness, as always, so now also Christ will be magnified in my body, whether by life or by death. (Phil. 1:20)

He hath shewed thee, O man, what is good; and what doth the LORD require of thee, but to do justly, and to love mercy, and to walk humbly with thy God? (Mic. 6:8)

And God *is* able to make all grace abound toward you, that you, always having all sufficiency in all *things*, may have an abundance for every good work. (2 Cor. 9:8)

Which scripture speaks to you the most and why?

____

____

____

____

____

A Daily Challenge for You

My daily challenge to you today is one of the best ones you can ever have! Do what God is telling you to do. Whatever He has put in your heart and in your spirit, take the next step, and move in your passion for Him today. Just seek His face first, write it down, put one of the scriptures above on it, and profess it each day. Then walk in your destiny! As He leads you, do something each day that causes you to live out your passion for Christ. I am so excited for you as this is going to be your best year yet!

My passion for Christ is to…

____

____

____

____

____

____

____

____

____

This, I profess in Jesus' name!

Daily Profession of the Word of God Transformed My Life This Week By...

A Sweet Place of Grace

There is a place of grace that you have to stay in during even the toughest of times. It is a sweet place where God gives you the strength to hold on and keeps you, so that you can see beyond your circumstances. It is during this time that you have to sacrifice your doubts and fears and realize the necessity of God's word to get you through it. Romans 5:3-5 says, *"Therefore being justified by faith, we have peace with God through our Lord Jesus Christ. By whom also we have access by faith into this grace, wherein we stand and rejoice in hope of the glory of God."* The awesome thing about this place of grace is that you enter it through your faith. And you can feel that grace when your faith is strengthened by listening to one of your favorite worship songs unto God, or kneeling at 5:00 a.m. in the morning, when everyone else is sleeping. You can also find it in the lifting of your hands when you have nothing else to say and, most of all, in the profession of God's word when you are telling the enemy to flee. Whatever the time or the test, just remember that through God's grace, He is doing something on the inside of you that will be a blessing for someone else. It is in this place of grace that God is causing you to stand, increasing your faith, and bringing you closer to Him!

Daily Profess God's Word for *A Sweet Place of Grace"*

Therefore, being justified by faith, we have peace with God through our Lord Jesus Christ. By whom also we have access by faith into this grace, wherein we stand and rejoice in hope of the glory of God. (Rom. 5)

For by grace you have been saved through faith, and that not of yourselves; *it is* the gift of God, not of works, lest anyone should boast. (Eph. 2:8)

But He gives more grace. Therefore, He says: "God resists the proud, but gives grace to the humble." (Jas 4:6)

Being justified freely by His grace through the redemption that is in Christ Jesus. (Rom. 3:24)

And He said to me, "My grace is sufficient for you, for My strength is made perfect in weakness." Therefore, most gladly I will rather boast in my infirmities, that the power of Christ may rest upon me." (2 Cor. 12:9)

What shall we say then? Shall we continue in sin that grace may abound? Certainly not! How shall we who died to sin live any longer in it? (Rom. 6:1-2)

You therefore, my son, be strong in the grace that is in Christ Jesus. (2 Tim. 2:1)

Which scripture speaks to you the most and why?

____

____

____

____

____

A Daily Challenge for You

I don't know about you, but I am so grateful for the grace that God has given me to be alive, forgiven, and strengthened, even though I have made mistakes. I want you to think about all that God has done for you, and how His grace has been abounding in your life. Start listing it down below. Then, give God praise and worship for how much He has done! I bet you will run out of space to write.

God has shown me love and given me grace by…

This, I profess in Jesus' name!

Daily Profession of the Word of God Transformed My Life This Week By...

Arise and Shine

Today is a *new* day! It is a day for you to leave behind your past and conquer your fears. It is a day to *step* out on faith, *believe*, and *trust God* like never before. And why not do so? Everything else changes anyway; people, jobs, circumstances in your day will always change. However, Jesus stays the same! Hebrews 13:8 says, *"Jesus Christ is the same, yesterday, today, and forever."* So, why not put your trust in Him and go forth! Declare that *today* is the day that I am going to *arise and shine!* I am going to allow the Son of God to arise in my life as I go from one place to the next and accomplish one task to the other. Isaiah 60:1 says, *"Arise and Shine; for the light has come! And the glory of the Lord is risen upon thee."*

Once you surrender to God's power and His plan and realize that you do not operate off man, you will see God's glory upon your life to do and accomplish anything He places in your spirit to do. Most of all, God says in His word that the glory of the Lord *is* risen upon thee not *has* risen upon thee. In other words, He is with you in the present, right now, shining His light upon the path He has set for you. So, do not be afraid of their faces, or what people say or think. Do not succumb to the fear of doubt or negative thoughts. "Choose ye this day whom you will serve," (Josh. 24:15) and let God order your steps. Declare healing, prosperity, wisdom, and direction; but most importantly, draw closer to Him by standing on His word and letting His glory shine through you as you are a witness for Him! This I profess over your life in Jesus' name!

Daily Profess God's Word and *Arise and Shine*

> Jesus Christ is the same, yesterday, today, and forever. (Heb. 13:8)

> And if it seems evil to you to serve the Lord, choose for yourselves this day whom you will serve, whether the gods which your fathers served that *were* on the other side of the River, or the gods of the Amorites, in whose land you dwell. But as for me and my house, we will serve the Lord. (Josh. 24:15)

> Arise and Shine; for the light has come! And the glory of the Lord is risen upon thee. For behold, the darkness shall cover the earth, and deep darkness the people; but the Lord will arise over you, and His glory will be seen upon you. (Is. 60:1-2)

And He said to him, "Arise, go your way. Your faith has made you well." (Lk 17:19)

Arise, walk in the land through its length and its width, for I give it to you. (Gen. 13:17)

For you were once darkness, but now *you are* light in the Lord. Walk as children of light. (Eph. 5:8)

Jesus said unto him, Rise, take up your bed, and walk. (Jn 5:8)

Which scripture speaks to you the most and why?

____

____

____

____

____

A Daily Challenge for You

It is time for you to *arise and shine!* You can no longer sit on your laurels and let the gifts God has given you lie dormant.

God has a calling on your life and created you for a divine purpose. Whatever it is, decide today that you are to operate in those gifts to your highest potential. Begin to write down a plan to get up and move forth in your destiny like never before. God is waiting to show it to you!

I will *arise and shine* this week and use my gifts for God's glory by…

____

____

____

____

____

____

____

____

____

____

____

This, I profess in Jesus' name!

Daily Profession of the Word of God Transformed My Life This Week By…

Be Spiritually Minded

It just does not pay to get caught up in what other people say or do that you may disagree with. People's actions can control how you feel, think, react, and behave if you let it. And before you know it, you will find yourself overwhelmed with emotion, consumed with negative thoughts, and your spirit is vexed because of what someone else said or did. Romans 8:6 says, *"For to be carnally minded is death but to be spiritually minded is life and peace."* Our flesh is going to naturally react to whatever tries to come against it. However, if we are spiritually minded, we will look beyond what is spoken or done and see the enemy's plans and the spiritual warfare behind it. At that point, we can choose to be carnally minded and react with our emotions and our flesh, or we can choose to be spiritually minded and see the victory that God has given us over it, which will give us life and peace! Being spiritual will give us life that helps us see how Jesus would handle it; life that will cause us to forgive because God has forgiven us. It will also give us peace that surpasses all understanding (Philippians 4:7) so that we can see God's plan through it all, and pray for the ones who persecute us.

How God sees us is most important, and if we keep that at the forefront of our minds, hearts, and spirits, we will be joyous in the fact that God will take care of the rest as we stay safe in His arms!

Daily Profess God's Word to *Be Spiritually Minded*

For they that are after the flesh do mind the things of the flesh; but they that are after the Spirit the things of the Spirit. (Rom. 8:5)

For to be carnally minded is death; but to be spiritually minded is life and peace. (Rom. 8:6)

Because the carnal mind is enmity against God: for it is not subject to the law of God, neither indeed can be. (Rom. 8:7)

But I see another law in my members, warring against the law of my mind, and bringing me into captivity to the law of sin which is in my members. (Rom. 7:23)

I thank God through Jesus Christ our Lord. So then with the mind I myself serve the law of God, but with the flesh the law of sin. (Rom. 7:25)

Therefore gird up the loins of your mind, be sober, and hope to the end for the grace that is to be brought unto you at the revelation of Jesus Christ. (1 Pet. 1:13)

And thou shall love the Lord thy God with all thy heart, and with all thy soul, and with all thy mind, and with all thy strength: this is the first commandment. (Mk 12:30)

These were more noble than those in Thessalonica, in that they received the word with all readiness of mind, and searched the scriptures daily, whether those things were so. (Acts 17:11)

And he that search the hearts knows what is the mind of the Spirit, because He makes intercession for the saints according to the will of God. (Rom. 8:27)

And be not conformed to this world: but be ye transformed by the renewing of your mind, that ye may prove what is that good, and acceptable, and perfect, will of God. (Rom. 12:2)

Which scripture speaks to you the most and why?

____

____

____

____

____

____

____

____

____

A Daily Challenge for You

You have to make a decision, before the attack or the disappointment comes, that you are going to keep your mind on God. People are always going to say and do things at times that will try and detour you from your focus on what God has called you to do. However, there is nothing like putting all of your trust in God, and declaring that you will have the mind of Christ so that you can move on and not be dismayed.

When warfare comes, I will be spiritually minded by…

This, I profess in Jesus' name!

Daily Profession of the Word of God Transformed My Life This Week By…

Be You

What makes you who you are? Are you funny, adventurous, quiet, or shy? And if someone was to ask you, are you being who you truly are, could you answer? I just recently traveled back to my home state of Arizona. And when I saw the mountains as I was looking out of the airplane window, I thought to myself *I am home, and this is a part of who I am.* You can look at the elements and ask, *How is that a part of someone?* However, when I got off the plane, took in the light, crisp, fresh air, gazed at the bright, blue sky and saw the mountains all around, I realized that this is why I am an optimist and a dreamer. No mountain has ever seemed too big for me because I always look up and see the beautiful expanse of the heavens and say, "God made this." So, if He has the power to make this, then I can overcome any mountain or obstacle with His strength.

This helped build my faith because I am a believer, a warrior, and I know my God is able. That's what my parents ingrained in me, but I have found out for myself that He is real and true. So, I can walk in my calling. I can be who God has called me to be. I can be the helpmate, the mother, the pastor's wife, the minister, the author, and the songwriter that He has ordained me to be. I can be me;

a silly, fun-loving, confident, optimistic, lover of the king, who loves a good black movie, and spending time with my family and sisters in Christ! So, I want to encourage you to "Be You." Psalm 139:14 says, *"I am fearfully and wonderfully made."*

God made you who you are and that is amazing! Just like the mountains, He created you to be great. So, just be you and don't lessen your faith in God for anyone or anything!

Daily Profess God's Word and *Be You*

I praise you because I am fearfully and wonderfully made. Wonderful are your works and my soul knows it very well. (Ps. 139:14-15)

The Lord does not look at my appearance or the height of my stature. He does not see as man sees me on the outward appearance, but He looks on my heart. (1 Sam. 16:7)

For I am His workmanship, created in Christ Jesus for good works which God prepared beforehand that I should walk in them. (Eph. 2:10)

Charm is deceitful and beauty is vain, but a woman who fears the Lord is to be praised. (Prov. 31:30)

Though an army encamp against me, my heart shall not fear; though war rise against me, yet I will be confident. (Ps. 27:3)

For everything created by God is good, and nothing is to be rejected if it is received with thanksgiving. (1 Tim. 4:4)

God created me in His own image, in the image of God He created me. (Gen. 1:27)

Which scripture speaks to you the most and why?

____

____

____

____

____

A Daily Challenge for You

It is time for you to just be yourself and be who God created you to be. This means that you do not have to change who you are based upon who you are around. You do not have to try and be someone else in order to fit in or to feel like you belong. This week, find out more about yourself and just be who God has called you to be. You are a loved child of the King who is more than a conqueror through Jesus Christ. So, enjoy being you, pay close attention to what makes you special, and why you do what you do. As long as you live by God's word and just be who God has created you to be, you will realize that you are fearfully and wonderfully made!

What is special about me being me is...

____

____

____

____

____

____

____

____

____

____

This, I profess in Jesus' name!

Daily Profession of the Word of God Transformed My Life This Week By...

Birthing the Extraordinary

When you are carrying something of value, you just don't give it to anyone or let them hold it. You protect it. You take care of it. You do whatever it takes to make sure it is covered. In the same way, when you are carrying what God has purposed you to do and know you are birthing something extraordinary, you cannot just hang around anyone or just do anything. You have to make sure you take care of what God has designed you to carry out, and allow God to place you only around people that will lift you up, affirm what God is doing in you, and hold you accountable to bring it forth. In other words, these people will always speak life to your purpose, tell you right from wrong, rejoice with you, and encourage you to be faithful to God and what He is calling you to do. Mary had this in Elisabeth when she was carrying baby Jesus. For in Luke 1:41-42 says *"And it came to pass, that, when Elisabeth heard the salutation of Mary, the babe leaped in her womb; and Elisabeth was filled with the Holy Ghost. And she spake out with a loud voice, said, Blessed art thou among women, and blessed is the fruit of thy womb."*

Elisabeth spoke life into Mary and encouraged her. Despite the fear or doubt that Mary had about carrying the Son of God, Elisabeth affirmed that Mary was chosen to do so! Because of that, Mary declared, "My soul doth magnify the Lord and my spirit hath rejoiced in God my Savior. For he hath regarded the low estate of his handmaiden: for, behold, from henceforth all generations shall call me blessed. For he that is mighty hath done to me great things; and holy is his name." (Lk 1:46-49). So, make sure you follow God and are attached to people who God has ordained to lift you up so that you can birth the extraordinary in your life!

Daily Profess God's Word for "*Birthing the Extraordinary*"

> And it came to pass, that when Elisabeth heard the salutation of Mary, the babe leaped in her womb; and Elisabeth was filled with the Holy Ghost. And she spake out with a loud voice, said, Blessed art thou among women, and blessed is the fruit of thy womb. (Lk 1:41-42)

> My soul doth magnify the Lord and my spirit hath rejoiced in God my Savior. For he hath regarded the low estate of his handmaiden: for, behold, from henceforth all generations shall call me blessed. For he that is mighty hath done to me great things; and holy is his name. (Lk 1:46-49)

But as many as received Him, to them, He gave the right to become children of God, even to those who believe in His name, who were born, not of blood nor of the will of the flesh nor of the will of man, but of God. (Jn 1:12-13)

In the exercise of His will He brought us forth by the word of truth, so that we would be a kind of first fruits among His creatures. (Jas 1:18)

Before I formed thee in the belly I knew thee; and before thou camest forth out of the womb I sanctified thee, and I ordained thee a prophet unto the nations. (Jer. 1:5)

If you know that He is righteous, you know that everyone also who practices righteousness is born of Him. (1 Jn 2:29)

Blessed be the God and Father of our Lord Jesus Christ, who according to His great mercy has caused us to be born again to a living hope through the resurrection of Jesus Christ from the dead. (1 Pet. 1:3)

I can do all things through Christ who strengthens me. (Phil. 4:13)

> Ye are of God, little children, and have overcome them: because greater is he that is in you, than he that is in the world. (1 Jn 4:4)

Which scripture speaks to you the most and why?

____

____

____

____

____

____

A Daily Challenge for You

I am so excited for you! I know there is something that God has placed in your spirit to do, or a gift that He has given you that you know you need to bring forth. So, put yourself in position to birth it out this week by spending time with God to hear His voice through His word on it. Surround yourself and share what God has spoken to you with people who will speak life into you and hold you accountable to fulfill it. Then watch God birth the extraordinary in your life!

The extraordinary thing, gift, business, or talent that God wants me to birth is…

This, I profess in Jesus' name!

Daily Profession of the Word of God Transformed My Life This Week By…

Break Out!

Have you ever just wanted to break out of something? You feel overwhelmed, bogged down, overcome with emotion, and you see no way out! You feel uncomfortable, uneasy, and there is something on the inside of you that wants to cry out. Well, one day, my son was making a fort, and he decided to pile all of the pillows on top of himself like he was buried so he could not get out. Immediately, my rescue mentality kicked in. My human survival instinct wanted to tell him "Break out of there!" And I realized, at that moment, that I needed to break out of the mental rut that I was in. I don't have to feel overwhelmed by circumstances, and I don't have to be bogged down by my own emotions. I can, through Christ, break out of this thing. 1 John 2:4 says *"He that saith, I know him, and keepeth not his commandments, is a liar, and the truth is not in him."* And I know that God has said that I am more than a conqueror through Christ Jesus.

Therefore, I need to keep His commandments and stop living a lie that I am trapped in my circumstances. The truth is in me, and I know I am going to break out! I know who my God is, and I do not have to believe the lie of the enemy that I am bound. So, I speak life unto you as well, right now, in the name of Jesus! Believe that God has given you the power to overcome any situation or circumstance you are in. Keep His commandments and do not let the enemy or even yourself hold you down or back any longer. Like my son eventually broke out of those pillows on top of him and roared with a smile, I challenge you today to break out of what you have been in, and break forth into your destiny!

Daily Profess God's Word and *Break Out*

> He that saith, I know him, and keepeth not his commandments, is a liar, and the truth is not in him. (1 Jn 2:4)

> I will say of the Lord, He is my refuge and my fortress: my God; in him will I trust. Surely he shall deliver you from the snare of the fowler, and from the deadly pestilence. (Ps. 91:2-3)

> For you have delivered my soul from death: will not you deliver my feet from falling, that I may walk before God in the light of the living? (Ps. 56:13)

> For you have delivered my soul from death, my eyes from tears, and my feet from falling. (Ps. 116:8)

For great *is* thy mercy toward me: and thou hast delivered my soul from the lowest hell. (Ps. 86:13)

You, Lord, brought me up from the realm of the dead; you spared me from going down to the pit. (Ps. 30:3)

He brought them out of darkness, the utter darkness, and broke away their chains. (Ps. 107:14)

Nay, in all these things we are more than conquerors through him that loved us. (Rom. 8:37)

Which scripture speaks to you the most and why?

____

____

____

____

____

A Daily Challenge for You

You are more than a conqueror through Christ who loves and gave His life for you. You are an overcomer! You are the head and not the tail, above and not beneath! And greater is He that is within you than He that is in the world! That is the truth. The word is what you should live by every day. So no matter how strong the attack gets, or how deep you think you are in your sin, remember God's word, stay humble, and obey His commandments, do what He says, and He will bring you out in Jesus's name! Now, profess His word every day and watch God break you out!

Today, I break out of __________________________ by professing that…

____

____

____

____

____

____

____

____

____

____

This, I profess in Jesus' name!

Daily Profession of the Word of God Transformed My Life This Week By...

Command Your Day

There is nothing like the time of the present. The past is gone away, and the future is yet to come. However, the present is here, right here, right now. So, you might as well enjoy it! You just have to ask yourself, what am I going to do with it? How am I going to live it? Am I going to let life pass me by, or am I going to "grab the bull by its horns" as they say, and make my mark in this world? The biggest way you can do that is by speaking God's word. Jesus said in John 6:63 that *"The words that I speak to you, they are spirit and they are life."* In other words, he was saying there is power in the words that I speak to bring life to a dead situation. I am Jesus, 100 percent human, yet 100 percent fully divine as the Son of God. Therefore, I know what I speak now will bring life to come.

So what are you going to speak? Command your day. Set the precedence before your day even starts. You can declare God's word over your situation and circumstance and say this is going to be a great day! And I will do what God is calling me to do. Like He said in Isaiah 55:8, *"My thoughts are not your thoughts, neither are my ways your ways, saith the Lord."* Therefore, you can declare, "Lord you are omniscient, all-knowing. I know that you can see beyond what I see so I know it is going to be an *awesome* day as I follow you. On this day, I will obey you and allow you to order my steps." It is amazing when you can proclaim that "this is the day that the Lord has made, I will rejoice and be glad in it." Whatever it is you have to declare over your day, do so, and watch the joy of the Lord be your strength right now! You have to command His word and say, "I will have peace. I will have joy, and I will not be defeated in Jesus's name!"

Daily Profess God's Word and *Command Your Day*

The words that I speak to you, they are spirit and they are life. (Jn 6:63)

My thoughts are not your thoughts, neither are my ways your ways, saith the Lord. For *as* the heavens are higher than the earth, so are my ways higher than your ways, and my thoughts than your thoughts. (Is. 55:8-9)

This is the day that the Lord has made; we will rejoice and be glad in it." (Ps. 118:24)

And the Lord shall make you the head, and not the tail; and you shall be above only, and you shall not be beneath; if that you hearken unto the commandments of the LORD your God, which I command you this day, to observe and to do them. (Deut. 28:13)

For the LORD your God will bless you as he has promised, and you will lend to many nations but will borrow from none. You will rule over many nations but none will rule over you. (Deut. 15:6)

Trust in the LORD with all your heart; and lean not unto your own understanding. In all your ways acknowledge him, and he shall direct your paths. (Prov. 3:5-6)

Jesus said unto him, You shall love the Lord your God with all your heart, and with all your soul, and with all your mind. (Matt. 22:37)

Which scripture speaks to you the most and why?

____

____

____

____

____

A Daily Challenge for You

You have to let God be the head of your life and take control of your day before you even start. This week, make it a point each day to profess His word over your life. Whatever scripture comes to mind, declare it, write it down, and be encouraged to walk in the promises of God throughout the day, no matter what comes your way. God wants to manifest His power through your faith in His word like never before! Daily, you will see your life transform.

When I profess your Word each day, I see…

____

____

____

____

____

____

____

____

____

This, I profess in Jesus' name!

Daily Profession of the Word of God Transformed My Life This Week By...

Declare, "I Will..."

In this day and time, we have to be definitive in our stance and firm in the decisions we make. It is so easy to be swayed to the left or to the right and follow the wrong thing because everyone else is doing it. However, you have to make up in your mind and say, "I will follow God, no matter what." It does not matter what people say or think or even how you feel. You must say, "I will bless the LORD at all times: his praise shall continually be in my mouth." (Ps. 34:1). You must be firm in your spirit and say, "I will walk in your way and follow your commands." For Psalm 119:1 says, *"Blessed are the undefiled in the way, who walk in the law of the Lord."* This is something you have to profess daily, so that you can crucify your flesh daily and be obedient to God's will and not your own.

So, walk with confidence today. Walk with boldness today. Boldly declare, "I will follow you." He is waiting on you to profess His Word. And when you do, you will see the manifested blessings of God begin to overflow in your life. You will draw closer to Him. You will see Him. You will see the promises of God come to life so that you can be a witness to others about what God can do! This I profess in Jesus's name!

Daily Profess God's Word and *Declare, "I will..."*

I will bless the Lord at all times: his praise shall continually be in my mouth. (Ps. 34:1)

I will pay my vows unto the Lord now in the presence of all his people, in the courts of the Lord's house, in the midst of you, O Jerusalem. Praise you the Lord. (Ps. 116:18-19)

I will love the Lord my God and keep His charge, His statutes, His rules, and His commandments always. (Deut. 11:1)

I will say of the Lord, He is my refuge and my fortress: my God; in him will I trust. (Ps. 91:2)

Blessed are the undefiled in the way, who walk in the law of the Lord. (Ps. 119:1)

A man's heart plans his way, but the Lord directs his steps. (Prov. 16:9)

The steps of a good man are ordered by the Lord, and He delights in his way. (Ps. 37:23)

I will extol you, my God, O king; and I will bless your name forever and ever. (Ps. 145:1)

> Behold, God is my salvation; I will trust, and not be afraid: for the LORD GOD is my strength and my song; he also has become my salvation. (Is. 12:2)

Which scripture speaks to you the most and why?

____

____

____

____

____

A Daily Challenge for You

Once you make up your mind to follow God, there is nothing or no one that can stop you. When you realize that He created you, walks and talks with you, and loves you unconditionally, you cannot help but trust Him and commit to being obedient to the purpose and plan for your life. So, make your declarations as to how you will live and serve the Lord. Remember, the power of life and death is in the tongue (Proverbs 18:21). This will help you move forward daily as you declare His promises, and how you will respond to what He has called you to do.

I declare I will…

This, I profess in Jesus' name!

Daily Profession of the Word of God Transformed My Life This Week By…

Draw Nigh unto Him

There is a love that the Father has for you that no one else can give. You can see it in the way He watches over you, keeps you, and provides for you. You can hear it in a song of worship or a melody of praise. You feel His presence when you need Him, call His name, fall on your knees, or even when you sit still in His presence and just breathe for a moment. It is a love so dear that He gave His only begotten Son so that you could be in relationship with Him as child of God. I used to recite John 3:16 all the time as a child, but when you really reflect upon His word, it tells the depth of His love for us: *"For God so loved the world that He gave His only begotten Son that whosoever believes in Him shall not perish but have everlasting life."*

I don't know which part of that verse touches you, but each part of it tells us of a different part of His character. Oh, He loves us so! He will give up what is most dear to him to bring us back to Him. He opens His arms so that anyone can believe in His Son. Then through Jesus's sacrifice, by dying on the cross and rising again, He gave us power over death, victory over sin and bondage, and the inheritance of eternal life with Him forever. So, why not run to Him? Why not draw nigh to Him in prayer, in worship, in the posture of raising your hands, or even in the yearning of your heart for more of who He is, when nothing on this earth can do. He is waiting for you to draw near to Him, even in silence so that you can Hear His voice. He wants you to feel the warmth of His presence, to cleanse you from your sins, and show you even more of His love! Just draw nigh unto Him and He will draw nigh to you (Jas 4:8).

Daily Profess God's Word and *Draw Nigh unto Him*

> Draw nigh to God, and he will draw nigh to you. Cleanse *your* hands, *ye* sinners; and purify *your* hearts, *ye* double minded. (Jas 4:8)
>
> Ho! Everyone who thirsts, come to the waters; And you who have no money come, buy and eat Come, buy wine and milk Without money and without cost. Why do you spend money for what is not bread, and your wages for what does not satisfy? Listen carefully to Me, and eat what is good, And delight yourself in abundance. Incline your ear and come to Me Listen, that you may live; And I will make an everlasting covenant with you, according to the faithful mercies shown to David. (Is. 55:1-3)

Seek the LORD while He may be found; Call upon Him while He is near. Let the wicked forsake his way and the unrighteous man his thoughts; And let him return to the LORD, And He will have compassion on him, And to our God, For He will abundantly pardon. (Is. 55:6-7)

And you said: Surely the LORD our God has shown us His glory and His greatness, and we have heard His voice from the midst of the fire. We have seen this day that God speaks with man; yet he *still* lives. (Deut. 5:24)

How blessed is the one whom You choose and bring near to You to dwell in Your courts. We will be satisfied with the goodness of Your house, Your holy temple. (Ps. 65:4)

The LORD is near to all who call upon Him, to all who call upon Him in truth. (Ps. 145:18)

Therefore, brethren, since we have confidence to enter the holy place by the blood of Jesus, by a new and living way which He inaugurated for us through the veil, that is, His flesh, and since we have a great priest over the house of God, let us draw near with a sincere heart in full assurance of faith, having our hearts sprinkled clean from an evil conscience and our bodies washed with pure water. (Heb. 10:19-22)

> Therefore say to them, "Thus says the LORD of hosts, 'Return to Me,' declares the LORD of hosts, 'that I may return to you,' says the LORD of hosts." (Zech. 1:3)

Which scripture speaks to you the most and why?

____

____

____

____

____

A Daily Challenge for You

God is waiting for you! He longs to be close to you. He made you to be close to Him, to have the breath of His life flowing through your veins. He wants you to draw nigh unto Him. He so desires for you to know and love Him more. So, go after Him. With abandonment, leave everything else behind and focus your mind on Him.

Cling to His word and Let Him fill you up with His love and His plans for your life. There is so much He has purposed for you. So, this week, put Him first like never before. Run to the very One who loves you so much.

Then stay there in His presence throughout your days so that you can hear Him and know what to do.

God, when I drew nigh unto you, you said…

This, I profess in Jesus' name!

Daily Profession of the Word of God Transformed My Life This Week By...

Enjoy Your Day!

Have you ever had the feeling in the midst of chaos that everything was going to be just fine? I know it sounds weird, and to be honest, it doesn't make much sense. However, in the midst of a busy morning getting the kids ready for school, and all that was on my plate to do as a wife, a mother, church administrator, business owner, and an author, I had this awakening yet small moment when the Holy Spirit said to me, "Enjoy the day!" And I realized at that moment how consumed I was and how it could be so much worse! I really did not have much to complain about because I am alive and here to do what I do. And guess what? Enjoy it! We can be such selfish human beings sometimes, with tunnel vision on how our day or our life is, and have the boldness to look at the world and everything going on around us through that same lens. However, the sun is still shining, the birds are still chirping, and God has graciously granted us another day to live! Psalm 118:24 says, *"This is the day that the Lord has made; we will rejoice and be glad in it."*

So, enjoy your day today. Don't look at the many details of life and what your day might entail and forget to remember that you are blessed to be here to see it. Take a deep breath, make sure you smile, enjoy the people God has placed around you, and most of all, give God praise for letting you see another day!

Daily Profess God's Word and *Enjoy Your Day!*

This is the day that the Lord has made; we will rejoice and be glad in it. (Ps. 118:24)

Behold that which I have seen: it is good and fitting for one to eat and to drink, and to enjoy the good of all his labor that he takes under the sun all the days of his life, which God gives him: for this is his lot. (Eccles. 5:18)

There is nothing better for a man, than that he should eat and drink, and the he should make his soul enjoy good in his labor. This also I saw, that it was from the hand of God. (Eccles. 2:24)

A merry heart does good like a medicine: but a broken spirit dries the bones. (Prov. 17:22)

All the days of the afflicted are evil: but he that is of a merry heart has a continual feast. (Prov. 15:15)

For he that will love life, and see good days, let him refrain his tongue from evil, and his lips that they speak deceit. (1 Pet. 3:10)

Until now have you asked nothing in my name: ask, and you shall receive, that your joy may be full. (Jn 16:24)

Charge them that are rich in this present age, that they be not haughty, nor trust in uncertain riches, but in the living God, who gives us richly all things to enjoy. (1 Tim. 6:17)

Blessed are you that hunger now: for you shall be filled. Blessed are you that weep now: for you shall laugh. (Lk 6:21)

You will show me the path of life: in your presence is fullness of joy; at your right hand there are pleasures forevermore. (Ps. 16:11)

Which scripture speaks to you the most and why?

____

____

____

____

____

____

____

____

____

A Daily Challenge for You

Make a decision today to enjoy your day in some way. It may be watching your favorite TV show, getting a scoop of ice cream, or just taking a minute to walk outside and just look at the sky, the trees, and take in the fresh air. However, whatever you do, remember that your time with God in His presence, through prayer, reading His word, or even through music of praise and worship unto Him, will be the only thing that can and will keep your joy full!

I will enjoy my day by…

This, I profess in Jesus' name!

Daily Profession of the Word of God Transformed My Life This Week By...

Expect God to Do Something Great!

It is time to experience what God has for us...*every day*. We have so much to be thankful for, so much to be grateful for. We have a God who loves us, cares for us, and provides for us. He wraps His arms around us, even when we don't deserve it. He surrounds us with His angels even when we turn the other way, and He continues to bless us even though we are not worthy of it. One thing I realized in August and September, when summer break is coming to an end, the kids are going back to school, and fall is on the way, there is an overall expectation that God still wants to do something new in our children. Like the expectation we have for our kids to have a great year, we need to *expect God* to start something fresh in us! Like a seed in the midst of soil, we have to be willing to rest in the very One who created us in order for it to come forth. God has so much in store for us! He wants to grow what He has planted in us, but we've got to let Him water us with His word, so that what He has ordained can harvest from within. He says in Psalm 1:2-3 that *blessed* is the man whose *"delight is in the law of the Lord, and in His law doth He meditate day and night. And he shall be like a tree planted by the rivers of water, that brings forth its fruit in its season; his leaf also shall not wither; and whatsoever he does shall prosper."* So, rest in Him. Stay planted in His word. Expect Him to do something great in you so that you can see the promises of God come to pass in your life this year!

Daily Profess God's Word and *Expect God to Do Something Great!*

But his delight is in the law of the LORD, and in His law he meditates day and night. He shall be like a tree planted by the rivers of water, that brings forth its fruit in its season; whose leaf also shall not wither; and whatsoever he does shall prosper. (Ps. 1:2-3)

My soul, wait thou only upon God; for my expectation is from him. (Ps. 62:5)

Only be thou strong and very courageous, that thou may observe to do according to all the law, which Moses my servant commanded you: turn not from it to the right hand or to the left, that thou may prosper wherever you go. (Josh. 1:7)

For surely there is an end; and thine expectation shall not be cut off. (Prov. 23:18)

And he gave heed unto them, expecting to receive something of them. (Acts 3:5)

According to my earnest expectation and my hope, that in nothing I shall be ashamed, but that with all boldness, as always, so now also Christ shall be magnified in my body, whether it be by life, or by death. (Phil. 1:20)

So shall the knowledge of wisdom be unto thy soul: when thou hast found it, then there shall be a reward, and thy expectation shall not be cut off. (Prov. 24:14)

And God is able to make all grace abound toward you; that ye, always having all sufficiency in all things, may abound to every good work. (2 Cor. 9:8)

Be careful for nothing; but in everything by prayer and supplication with thanksgiving let your requests be made known unto God. (Phil. 4:6)

Which scripture speaks to you the most and why?

____

____

____

____

____

____

____

____

____

A Daily Challenge for You

We can make a choice to both get stuck and accept life how it is, or we can choose to put our expectation in God, in what He has for us, and move forward! So why not expect God to do something great? Why not have faith in Him to do the impossible? How will not believing help you, anyway? So, instead of settling for the mundane, redundant, ordinary life, depend upon His word, profess His promises, and watch God exceed your expectations on a daily basis!

I expect God to...

This, I profess in Jesus' name!

Daily Profession of the Word of God Transformed My Life This Week By…

Fullness of Joy Just for You!

In this day and time, you have to know where your joy comes from. You have to know that it does not just come from the child you love, the person you work with, the friends you hang out with, or the spouse you adore. It comes from the One who is all around you, who covers you, and protects you. We were created to glorify Him. We were designed to serve Him. We were made to experience the fullness of joy that only He can give. Because of this, I have made up my mind to stay right next to Him; to stay in His presence and trust Him as my source for everything. For Jesus said in John 15:4 *"Abide in me, and I in you. As the branch cannot bear fruit of itself, except it abide in the vine; no more can ye, except ye abide in me."* This is what we have to remember so that we will have the joy and peace He wants to freely give us every day and be all that God has ordained us to be. He is our source and He is our joy! So, why not stay in His presence by believing in His Word despite what comes our way. For Jesus said, *"These things have I spoken unto you, that my joy might remain in you, and that your joy might be full."* (Jn 15:11). This I pray and declare for you in Jesus' name!

Daily Profess God's Word for *"Fullness of Joy Just for You!"*

Abide in me, and I in you. As the branch cannot bear fruit of itself, except it abide in the vine; no more can ye, except ye abide in me. (Jn 15:4)

These things have I spoken unto you, that my joy might remain in you, and that your joy might be full. (Jn 15:11)

Rejoicing in hope; patient in tribulation; continuing instant in prayer. (Rom. 12:12)

Now the God of hope fill you with all joy and peace in believing, that ye may abound in hope, through the power of the Holy Ghost. (Rom. 15:13)

Hitherto have ye asked nothing in my name: ask, and ye shall receive, that your joy may be full. (Matt. 16:24)

But the fruit of the Spirit is love, joy, peace, longsuffering, gentleness, goodness, faith. (Gal. 5:22)

For the kingdom of God is not meat and drink; but righteousness, and peace, and joy in the Holy Ghost. (Rom. 14:17)

And ye now therefore have sorrow: but I will see you again, and your heart shall rejoice, and your joy no man taketh from you. (Jn 16:22)

Therefore, my heart is glad, and my glory rejoiceth: my flesh also shall rest in hope. (Ps. 16:9)

Rejoice evermore. (1 Thess. 5:16)

Which scripture speaks to you the most and why?

____

____

____

____

____

A Daily Challenge for You

The Bible says that *"the steadfast love of the Lord never ceases, and that his mercies never come to an end; for they are new every morning; great is thy faithfulness"* (Lam. 3:22-23). So, if he has a clean slate for us every day, and a fresh dose of love and mercies that He wants to give us, why can't we look forward to the joy we have in Him every day? This week, make it a point to rest in the joy of knowing Him. When things come your way or issues arise, take a moment, call upon Him, and trust Him to give you the peace, wisdom, and joy to get through it. Experience the day He has for you and let nothing take that away!

I will experience the fullness of joy, despite what happens this week, by...

____

____

____

____

____

____

____

____

____

____

____

This, I profess in Jesus' name!

Daily Profession of the Word of God Transformed My Life This Week By…

Go Forth in Your Calling

God is calling us further in and deeper into His presence. This is not the time to be on the fence about your relationship with God. God is looking for believers who are willing to seek His face and do what He has called us to do. There are lives to be saved, people to be delivered, and captives to be set free. People who are captives to this world, captives to their situations or circumstances, need to hear the delivering power of Jesus Christ that can bring joy and peace in the midst of their storm. They need to know that they can have a life in Christ that frees them from sin, guilt, bondage, or the pain of their past. They need to know that there is the one and only God who loves them more than they could ever love themselves. Jesus told the disciples in Matthew 28:19: *"Go ye therefore and teach all nations, baptizing them in the name of the Father, the Son and of the Holy Ghost."* He wanted the world to know that He was sent to cleanse us, wash us of all iniquity, and save us from the sins of this world.

So, you have to ask yourself, what is your purpose? What has God called you to do? Where has He called you to be a witness? It is time for you to stay before Him in His word to hear what He is calling you to do, and where He is telling you to go? He has placed gifts and talents in you to be used for His glory so that every person He has ordained for you to be a light to will have an opportunity to know Him. My prayers are with you as you go forth in Jesus's name!

Daily Profess God's Word and *Go Forth in Your Calling*

Go ye therefore and teach all nations, baptizing them in the name of the Father, the Son and of the Holy Ghost. Teaching them to observe all things whatsoever I have commanded you: and, lo, I am with you always, even unto the end of the world. Amen. (Matt. 28:19-20)

I therefore, the prisoner of the Lord, beseech you that you walk worthy of the vocation by which you are called, with all lowliness and meekness, with longsuffering, forbearing one another in love; endeavoring to keep the unity of the Spirit in the bond of peace. (Eph. 4:3)

Therefore, rather, brethren, give diligence to make your calling and election sure: for if you do these things, you shall never fall. (2 Pet. 1:10)

For you see your calling, brethren, how that not many wise men after the flesh, not many mighty, not many noble, are called: But God has chosen the foolish things of the world to confound the wise; and God has chosen the weak things of the world to confound the things which are mighty. (1 Cor. 1:26-27)

Therefore, also we pray always for you, that our God would count you worthy of this calling, and fulfill all the good pleasure of His goodness, and the work of faith with power: that the name of our Lord Jesus Christ may be glorified in you, and you in Him, according to the grace of our God and the Lord Jesus Christ. (2 Thess. 1:11-12)

There is one body, and one Spirit, even as you are called in one hope of your calling. (Eph. 4:4)

Which scripture speaks to you the most and why?

___

___

___

___

___

A Daily Challenge for You

It is a wonderful thing to know that God loves you and has called you for a *great* purpose! He knows exactly what He has deposited in you and what you are capable of. Now, all you have to do is stay before Him in prayer, and in His word, so that He can give you the instruction you need to *go forth* in your calling! You have an amazing journey ahead of you and so many lives will be blessed and transformed because of your obedience to Him!

I will go forth in my calling by…

____

____

____

____

____

____

____

____

____

This, I profess in Jesus' name!

Daily Profession of the Word of God Transformed My Life This Week By...

God Will Do Wonders!

When God sees us, He sees immeasurable possibilities of His power in our lives. He sees fertile ground that His spirit can reside in, which is why He breathed the breath of life into Adam and He became a living soul (Genesis 2:7). And even when He made Adam fall into a deep sleep and pulled a rib out of his side to make Eve, a woman, who could continue to produce the life that He had created, He saw the ways His promises could manifest. So when God sees you, He sees who He has created, who He loves, and all that He has put on the inside of you to bring Him glory!

This is why you should have an expectation for God to do wonders among you. Every day, you should wake up and humble yourself before the Father in prayer, in worship, or in His Word, and believe God for what He wants to do in your life. He already did miracles through His Son Jesus Christ in giving us a way to have relationship with Him. So, why not live, move, and have our being in Him who created us to experience His presence and His power? Exodus 15:11 says, *"Who is like unto you, O Lord, among the gods? Who is like you, glorious in holiness, fearful in praises, doing wonders?"* We know how awesome God is, therefore, we must look to Him and expect Him to do wonders among us in ways unimaginable. He has already shown us His sovereignty. All we have to do is stay in His presence and follow His lead so we can see it and receive it!

Daily Profess God's Word, for *God Will Do Wonders!*

Who is like unto you, O LORD, among the gods? Who is like you, glorious in holiness, fearful in praises, doing wonders? (Exod. 15:11)

You are the God that does wonders: you have declared your strength among the people. (Ps. 77:14)

Many, O LORD my God, are your wonderful works which you have done, and your thoughts which are toward us: they cannot be recounted in order unto you: if I would declare and speak of them, they are more than can be numbered. (Ps. 40:5)

I would seek unto God, and unto God would I commit my cause: Who does great things and unsearchable; marvelous things without number. (Job 5:8-9)

O sing unto the Lord a new song; for He has done marvelous things: His right hand, and His holy arm, has gotten Him the victory. (Ps. 98:1)

I will declare His glory among the heathen; His marvelous works among all nations. (1 Chron. 16:24)

Blessed be the Lord God, the God of Israel, who only does wondrous things. And blessed be His glorious name forever: and let the whole earth be filled with His glory; Amen, and Amen. (Ps. 72:18-19)

All nations which you have made shall come and worship before you, O Lord; and shall glorify your name. For you are great, and do wondrous things; you are God alone. (Ps. 86:9-10)

O Lord, you are my God; I will exalt you, I will praise your name; for you have done wonderful things; your counsels of old are faithfulness and truth. (Is. 25:1)

And Joshua said unto the people, sanctify yourselves: for tomorrow the Lord will do wonders among you. (Josh. 3:5)

Which scripture speaks to you the most and why?

____

____

____

____

____

____

____

____

____

A Daily Challenge for You

From this day forward, lift up your eyes to the hills from which comes your help (Ps. 121:1). Look for God to move in immeasurable ways so that you can experience His power and His glory in everything you do. You may see Him move through the wind blowing through the trees, in the smile of someone you love, in the stars that shine in darkness, or even in the peace only He can give in the midst of a storm. Just make sure to declare His glory, humble yourself before Him each day, and expect God to do wonders among you!

I expect God to...

This, I profess in Jesus' name!

Daily Profession of the Word of God Transformed My Life This Week By…

Guard Your Heart

Whenever you are going higher in God, Satan will try and stop it. The more you grow in your faith, read God's word, and start living by it, the more you will see Satan come against you to try and distract you from it. We have to guard our hearts and protect our minds in the spirit realm so that we are not swayed by his tactics or strategies to bring us down. He may try and discourage you through a negative situation with a friend, or in trouble with a family member. He may even try to attack your body with physical illness to slow you down. However, just remember that Ephesians 6:12 says, *"For we wrestle not against flesh and blood, but against principalities, against powers, against the rulers of the darkness of this world, against spiritual wickedness in high places."* Therefore, we need to put on the Armor of God (Eph. 6:10-18) when it comes to our emotions, our minds, and our wills, which is what our hearts consists of. We've got to get to the soul of the matter and make sure we are not swayed by our emotions in circumstances that try to overwhelm us, protect our minds with His word when our thoughts want to run amuck, and profess His Word daily so that we can submit our wills to His will and follow God. We have got to guard our hearts, use His wisdom, and let Him defeat the enemy because the battle has already been won!

Daily Profess God's Word and *Guard Your Heart*

> Finally, my brethren, be strong in the Lord, and in the power of His might. Put on the whole armor of God, that ye may be able to stand against the wiles of the devil. (Eph. 6:10-11)

> For we wrestle not against flesh and blood, but against principalities, against powers, against the rulers of the darkness of this world, against spiritual wickedness in high places. (Eph. 6:12)

> For as he thinks in his heart, so is he: Eat and drink, says he to you; but his heart is not with you. (Prov. 23:7)

> Be anxious for nothing; but in everything by prayer and supplication with thanksgiving let your requests be made known unto God. And the peace of God, which passes all understanding, shall keep your hearts and minds through Christ Jesus. (Phil. 4:6-7)

> Create in me a clean heart, O God, and renew a right spirit within me. (Ps. 51:10)

> My flesh and my heart fails: but God is the strength of my heart, and my portion forever. (Ps. 73:26)

> Trust in the Lord with all your heart and lean not to your own understanding. In all your ways acknowledge Him, and He shall direct your paths. (Prov. 3:5-6)

Which scripture speaks to you the most and why?

____

____

____

____

____

A Daily Challenge for You

God gave you a heart so that it could belong to Him. There is no allegiance to anyone or anything that should take the place on the throne of your heart than Jesus. So, protect it. Guard it. And make sure that you are constantly humble and faithful to the One who gave you everlasting life! This week, make sure to examine your heart and see what is not of God. It also may be your love for someone else or something that you are putting before God. Even a family member, a friend, significant other, or your own personal desires can get in the way of total devotion to obey and do God's will in your life. Once you are honest with yourself, ask God to remove whatever it is that will hinder you from giving all of your heart to Him and guard your heart so that He can always be your first love.

I will guard my heart by…

___

___

___

___

___

___

___

___

___

___

___

This, I profess in Jesus' name!

Daily Profession of the Word of God Transformed My Life This Week By...

He Will Provide

There may be times when you feel like you are underwater financially or just overwhelmed by bills, expenses, and you feel like you are losing ground. However, God is clear in His word that He will provide! Ephesians 3:20 says, *"I will do exceedingly and abundantly above all you could ask or think according to the power that works within you."* It is all about your faith in God and what you are willing to do to be in position to receive it. First, you must make sure you seek Him first for wisdom and direction. Hebrews 11:6 says, *"But without faith it is impossible to please Him, for he who comes to God must believe that He is, and that He is a rewarder of those who diligently seek Him."* Then Matthew 6:33 says, *"Seek ye first the Kingdom of God, and His righteousness, and all these things shall be added unto you."* You will find that you must first give unto Him in your tithes, offering, and seed. If you give unto God, He will give unto you. Then as you use His wisdom to budget, pay off debt, and save, you need to profess His word for your prosperity. Many people underestimate the power of professing God's word. However, 2 Corinthians 1:20 says, *"For all the promises of God in him are yea, and in him Amen, unto the glory of God by us."*

You have to stand upon His word daily and hold fast to His promises. Some days, it may seem like it is taking a long time for things to come through, but God is faithful to what He has promised! This I profess in Jesus's name!

Daily Profess God's Word and *He Will Provide*

I will do exceedingly and abundantly above all you could ask or think according to the power that works within you. (Eph. 3:20)

But without faith it is impossible to please Him, for he who comes to God must believe that He is, and that He is a rewarder of those who diligently seek Him. (Heb. 11:6)

Seek ye first the Kingdom of God, and His righteousness, and all these things shall be added unto you. (Matt. 6:33)

If they obey and serve *him*, they shall spend their days in prosperity, and their years in pleasures. (Job 36:11)

Let them shout for joy, and be glad, that favour my righteous cause: yea, let them say continually, Let the Lord be magnified, which hath pleasure in the prosperity of his servant. (Ps. 35:27)

> The young lions do lack, and suffer hunger: but they that seek the LORD shall not lack any good thing. (Ps. 34:10)

> Be not therefore like them: for your Father knows what things you have need of, before you ask him. (Matt. 6:8)

Which scripture speaks to you the most and why?

____

____

____

____

____

A Daily Challenge for You

When my husband and I were believing God to increase our prosperity and provide in our finances, we made sure to seek His face, give obediently, and pay off our debt as best we could. And even when it got tough, we would continue to profess God's word. So, do not put your trust in man or in money. Start giving unto God, profess His word and His promises, and watch Him transform your financial situation in Jesus's name! There is one thing that God says in His word about finances. He says in Malachi 3:10, *"Bring ye all the tithes into the storehouse, that there may be meat in mine house, and prove me now herewith, saith the Lord of hosts, if I will not open you the windows of heaven, and pour you out a blessing, that there shall not be room enough to receive it."* Obey God and watch Him do what only He can do!

I believe God will provide…

____

____

____

____

____

____

____

____

____

____

____

This, I profess in Jesus' name!

Daily Profession of the Word of God Transformed My Life This Week By...

Jesus Loves Me

After celebrating Valentine's Day one year, I thought there is nothing like true love, a true friend, or somebody who loves you just for being you! There is nothing like when someone knows who you are and you do not have to hide anything from them. You can be yourself, let it all out, and not hold back. At the same time, that person knows you and will always help keep you on track, no matter what. They will tell you when you are wrong and when you are right, and will always look out for your best interest. If we can be real, this is the type of relationship that people long for, especially women because we can be such emotional beings, and we need a safe place and time to get it out.

As you are reading, you may be thinking about some of your best friends or brothers and sisters in Christ. However, I am talking about the living and breathing relationship you can have with Jesus Christ. There is a bond with Him that is undeniably the best relationship we could ever have! We just have to embrace Him and spend time with Him every day, like we would our closest friend. We have to remember that He loves us and wants to have a true relationship with us. *"For God so loved the world that He gave His only begotten Son that whosoever believeth in Him should not perish but have everlasting life"* (Jn 3:16). We have to remember that Jesus made the *ultimate sacrifice* and gave His life so that we could be *one* with Him and live *free* from every bondage, hurt, sin, or pain. Relationships are what can make or break us, tear us down, or make us stronger. This is why it is so important to build your relationship with Jesus Christ as the ultimate one and follow Him.

Daily Profess God's Word, "*Jesus Loves Me*"

For God so loved the world that He gave His only begotten Son that who so ever believes in him shall not perish but have everlasting life. (Jn 3:16)

Jesus said, "If you love me, you will keep my commandments." (Jn 14:15)

The Lord, a God merciful and gracious, slow to anger, and abounding in steadfast love and faithfulness. (Exod. 34:6)

I will not be anxious about anything, but by prayer and supplication, with thanksgiving, I will make my requests known unto God. And the peace of God which surpasses all understanding, will keep my heart and mind at rest in Christ Jesus. (Phil. 4:6-7)

I will humble myself, under God's mighty and He will lift me up. (1 Pet. 5:6)

Jesus said, "Peace I leave with you; my peace I give you. I do not give to you as the world gives. Do not let your hearts be troubled and do not be afraid." (Jn 14:27)

Lord, I cast all of my cares upon you for you care for me. (1 Pet. 5:7)

I will trust in the Lord with all my heart and lean not to my own understanding. In all my ways I will acknowledge Him and He will direct my paths. (Prov. 3:5-6)

Which scripture speaks to you the most and why?

____

____

____

____

____

____

____

A Daily Challenge for You

At the end of the day, life is about relationships. We can go to work, go to school, drive home, and make all the money in the world, but if we don't have relationship with those that we love, then it is meaningless. You enjoy the times you have with people who make you laugh and who will be there for you when you cry because they genuinely care about you. And God cares about you even more. He loves you even more because God is love (1 John 4:8). So, why is He not the closest relationship we have every day of our lives? Go ahead and enjoy Him, love Him, and give Him your all! He is waiting for you....

Jesus loves me, so I will…

This, I profess in Jesus' name!

Daily Profession of the Word of God Transformed My Life This Week By...

Let Go of Ties That Bind

It is hard to let go of someone or something that is holding you down or has held you back from being who God has called you to be. They or it has become a part of the fabric of your life, and you have learned to live with them being attached to it. So, when you are no longer attached, you literally go through a grieving process because you have lost something that, although it is harmful to you, it is still valuable to you. You have invested your love, dedication, and time into that person or thing and, therefore, the influence of it all is strong in your life. However, getting rid of the soul ties that bind is something that has to take place in order for you to grow and go higher in Christ. This person or situation will only make your life worse if you hold on to them because they produce nothing but the bad fruit of things, like doubt, confusion, fear, or depression.

This is when you know you need to cut it off because they taint your life with ungodly things, and you have put them before God. They rely on your ability to overcome strongholds, and make it seem as if you cannot live without them, when you have the yoke-destroying power of Jesus Christ in your life. 2 Corinthians 10:3-4 says, *"For though we walk in the flesh, we do not war according to the flesh:*

(For the weapons of our warfare are not carnal, but mighty through God to the pulling down of strongholds." So, let go of the ties that bind by letting God pull down those strongholds in your life. Commit yourself to follow God, even in your thoughts, and obey Christ. Receive the love, joy, and peace that comes from being in a fruitful relationship with Jesus so that you can move forward and live free to fulfill your destiny!

Daily Profess God's Word and *Let Go of Ties That Bind*

Every good tree bears good fruit, but a bad tree bears bad fruit. A good tree cannot bear bad fruit, nor can a bad tree bear good fruit. Every tree that does not bear good fruit is cut down and thrown into the fire. Therefore, by their fruits you will know them. (Matt. 7:17-20)

For though we walk in the flesh, we do not war according to the flesh: (For the weapons of our warfare are not carnal, but mighty through God to the pulling down of strongholds;). (2 Cor. 10:3-4)

Casting down arguments, and every high thing that exalts itself against the knowledge of God, and bringing into captivity every thought to the obedience of Christ. (2 Cor. 10:5)

Verily I say unto you, whatsoever you shall bind on earth shall be what has been bound in heaven: and whatsoever you shall loose on earth shall be what has been loosed in heaven. (Matt. 18:18)

Stand fast therefore in the liberty with which Christ has made us free, and be not entangled again with the yoke of bondage. (Gal. 5:1)

Which scripture speaks to you the most and why?

____

____

____

____

____

A Daily Challenge for You

You are going to have to learn on a daily basis to live for Christ and know that He is your source of joy, love, and peace; not the friend, relationship, or situation that you have to let go of. It is going to be important to speak His word against those strongholds and fill your spirit with good fruit so that the enemy can't return or make you hold on to what has bound you in the past. Just know that God knows what is best for you, so move forward, live free, and run after your destiny in Christ!

I will let go of ties that bind by...

____

____

____

____

____

____

____

____

____

____

____

This, I profess in Jesus' name!

Daily Profession of the Word of God Transformed My Life This Week By…

Life Is What You Make It... Enjoy It!

I am realizing now more than ever that life is precious, and it is what you make it. We have to take the time to enjoy the One who gave it to us, and the people we love!

There is nothing like peace in the morning, spending time with family, good food with great friends, and rest in His presence. There is nothing like being able to eat your favorite ice cream, watch your favorite show, or listen to your favorite song, especially when you know you have given your all.

The truth of the matter is that we have a choice to make every day. We can be overwhelmed, down, and depressed about our situation or circumstances, *or* we can be thankful, hopeful, and rejoice about the fact that God has given us life for another day! We need the peace that only He can give, and it is awaiting us every time we open our eyes. We just have to be intentional and grab hold of it. We have to spend time in prayer with God so we can hear His voice, give our all unto Him in what He has called us to do. We also have to make sure to balance the time needed to enjoy what He blessed us with in the first place. 1 Thessalonians 5:16-18 says it best *"Rejoice always, pray without ceasing, in everything give thanks; for this is the will of God in Christ Jesus for you."* This I profess in Jesus's name!

Daily Profess God's Word, *"Life Is What You Make It"*

Rejoice always, pray without ceasing, in everything give thanks; for this is the will of God in Christ Jesus for you. (1 Thess. 5:16-18)

There is nothing better for a man, than that he should eat and drink, and that he should make his soul enjoy good in his labor. This also I saw, that it was from the hand of God. (Eccles. 2:24)

For he that will love life, and see good days, let him refrain his tongue from evil, and his lips that they speak no guile: (1 Pet. 3:10)

Hitherto have ye asked nothing in my name: ask, and ye shall receive, that your joy may be full. (Jn 16:24)

And my spirit hath rejoiced in God my Saviour. (Lk 1:47)

A merry heart doeth good [like] a medicine: but a broken spirit drieth the bones. (Prov. 17:22)

I know that there is no good in them, but for a man to rejoice, and to do good in his life. And also that every man should eat and drink, and enjoy the good of all his labor, it is the gift of God. (Eccles. 3:12-13)

Which scripture speaks to you the most and why?

____

____

____

____

____

My Daily Challenge to You

Don't miss another day or moment that God has given you to enjoy. Be intentional! Find something that you love to do or that just makes you happy and make sure you do it. Every day, there should be some point where you take a deep breath and just rest in the fact that you are alive and in God's hands. You could spend a moment looking at the trees, laugh with your child, or just take a quick nap. Most of all, just be thankful that God has blessed you to see another day!

I will enjoy life every day by…

This, I profess in Jesus' name!

Daily Profession of the Word of God Transformed My Life This Week By…

Lift Up Your Head!

It is amazing to actually be in the dispensation of time that God has ordained; to actually see what He has spoken and live out the manifestation of His promises. Sometimes, we dream for so long, and we forget that God wants to bless us today! He wants us to experience heaven on earth right now! He wants to give us that peace and joy that we so desire. We just have to be willing to lift up our heads above our circumstances or situations and realize that, ultimately, God is in control. We were not created to live our lives to please other people or to look to man to bring our plans to fruition. We were created to glorify God and trust Him to be our provider. For Psalm 24:7 says, *"Lift up your heads, O you gates; and be you lifted up, you everlasting doors; and the King of glory shall come in."*

He is waiting to show himself strong. He is waiting to show us His power and the essence of who He is by raising us up against all odds so that He can get the glory. All we have to do is lift up our heads and know to whom we belong. We have got to know that there is nothing that can stop what God has planned for our lives, and He will help us even get over our own personal struggles so that what He has declared will come to pass. For "Who is this King of glory? The Lord strong and mighty, the Lord mighty in battle." (Ps. 24:8).

Daily Profess God's Word and *Lift Up Your Head!*

Lift up your heads, O you gates; and be you lifted up, you everlasting doors; and the King of glory shall come in. (Ps. 24:7)

Who is the King of glory? The Lord strong and mighty, the Lord mighty in battle. (Ps. 24:8).

Ah, Sovereign Lord, you have made the heavens and the earth by your great power and outstretched arm. Nothing is too hard for you. (Jer. 32:17)

I will lift up my eyes unto the hills, from which comes my help. My help comes from the Lord, who made heaven and earth. (Ps. 121:1)

And now shall my head be lifted up above my enemies round about me: therefore will I offer in his tabernacle sacrifices of joy; I will sing, yea, I will sing praises unto the Lord. (Ps. 27:6)

But you, O Lord, are a shield for me; my glory, and the lifter up of my head. (Ps. 3:3)

> Is not the LORD your God with you? and has he not given you rest. (1 Chron. 22:18)

> I will sing the LORD's praise, because He has dealt bountifully with me. (Ps. 13:6)

Which scripture speaks to you the most and why?

____

____

____

____

____

A Daily Challenge for You

When you wake up tomorrow in the morning, let the first thing that you say and do is to lift your hands and say, "Hallelujah!" Rejoice over the fact that God woke you up another day and get up, looking for how the king of glory will come in. Open your eyes to see His goodness and look for Him to move in a different way this week, in every situation, or circumstance. Know that He wants to show you His power, and He is just waiting on you to invite Him to do so. Lift up your head and the king of glory shall come in!

I will lift up my head because...

This, I profess in Jesus' name!

Daily Profession of the Word of God Transformed My Life This Week By...

Live Free and Experience God's Wonders!

I sometimes struggle with how often to write, battling in my mind what should be said or what shouldn't. It's how we feel in life sometimes. We wonder whether to reveal how we really feel or hold back and conceal it. However, I have just recently gotten to the point in life where I now realize that I need to be real with God every day and not be afraid to share what I am going through. I cannot hold back but share with others what it is to be free from even your own thoughts. I need to be real with God and not be afraid to be me, no matter who I am around. Life is too short, they say, but the reality is that life is abundant and full of time to experience the wonders of God that He has for us in it. So why hold back, fret, or worry what others will think? Why get caught up in our own fears and not live life the way God wants us to: free from sin and bondage? Exodus 15:11 says, *"Who is like unto you, O Lord, among the gods? Who is like you, glorious in holiness, fearful in praises, doing wonders?"* God is miraculous! And He is doing wonders every day, but we will miss it if we are bound by our own restraints. So, enjoy life! Don't be afraid to be real with Him, share with others as God leads, and live free of the ties that bind, especially in your mind. That is the miracle that He has given us through Jesus Christ, and we can live in that freedom every day. So, let's *live free* and experience the wonders of God as we draw closer to Him!

Daily Profess God's Word and *Live Free*

Who is like unto you, O Lord, among the gods? Who is like you, glorious in holiness, fearful in praises, doing wonders? (Exod. 15:11)

Now the Lord is that Spirit: and where the Spirit of the Lord is, there is liberty. (2 Cor. 3:17)

If the Son therefore shall make you free, you shall be free indeed. (Jn 8:36)

Stand fast therefore in the liberty with which Christ has made us free, and be not entangled again with the yoke of bondage. (Gal. 5:1)

For, brethren, you have been called unto liberty; only use not liberty for an occasion to the flesh, but by love serve one another. (Gal. 5:13)

You are the God that does wonders: you have declared your strength among the people. (Ps. 77:14)

For you are great, and do wondrous things: you are God alone. (Ps. 86:10)

Blessed be the LORD God, the God of Israel, who only does wondrous things. (Ps. 72:18)

To him who alone does great wonders: for his mercy endures forever. (Ps. 136:4)

Which scripture speaks to you the most and why?

____

____

____

____

____

A Daily Challenge for You

I am so excited for you because every day is a new day, and on this day, you can *live free* of anything that binds you. You cannot change the present. You can only control your future. So, *live free today*. Any ties that bind you or any sin that wants to keep you bound, sincerely confess it unto God. Focus on the fact that He is wondrous and powerful enough to have mercy on you, set you free, and give you the strength to walk in that freedom. Now, go forth in the liberty that He has given you, and experience the wonders of His love! Have a wonderfully blessed week!

I will live free and experience God's wonders by…

This, I profess in Jesus' name!

Daily Profession of the Word of God Transformed My Life This Week By…

Live in Peace

Have you ever been in a place where you are just not settled? Everything is going like clockwork in your life, but you're still a little uneasy. You get up in the morning, carry out your daily routines, and go about your day as usual, but there is still something in your spirit that is not right.

This is a warning sign that your personal time with God is much needed and overdue. God has given us intelligence, wisdom, and the ability to live out our days, but we sometimes get comfortable, cocky, and downright arrogant with it when we keep doing our own thing every day and never seek His face. We need to hear the voice of God. He did not give us our gifts and talents or the natural ability to accomplish our tasks and our goals to just turn around and deny Him with them. He gave them to us so that we would know how to draw closer to Him, and we could use them for His glory so that others may see Him through us. Romans 15:13 says, *"Now the God of hope fill you with all joy and peace in believing, that ye may abound in the hope, through the power of the Holy Ghost."* In other words, while we live this life in faith, He wants to fill us with His joy and peace so that we can abound in the power of the Holy Ghost in what we do daily!

So, let's spend more time with Him to seek His direction so that we can be filled each day with His peace instead of going through the motions or being overwhelmed. Our spirit man needs the very One who created us in order to be secure in who we are and truly enjoy the life of peace!

Daily Profess God's Word and *Live in Peace*

> Now the God of hope fill you with all joy and peace in believing, that ye may abound in the hope, through the power of the Holy Ghost. (Rom. 15:13)
>
> For God is not the author of confusion, but of peace, as in all churches of the saints. (1 Cor. 14:33)
>
> Let him eschew evil, and do good; let him seek peace, and ensue it. (1 Pet. 3:11)
>
> Thou will keep him in perfect peace, whose mind is stayed on thee: because he trusted in thee. (Is. 26:3)
>
> For to be carnally minded is death; but to be spiritually minded is life and peace. (Rom. 8:6)
>
> These things I have spoken unto you, that in me ye might have peace. In the world ye shall have tribulation: but be of good cheer; I have overcome the world. (Jn 16:33)

Therefore, being justified by faith, we have peace with God through our Lord Jesus Christ. (Rom. 5:1)

The LORD make His face shine upon you, and be gracious unto you: The LORD lift up His countenance upon you, and give you peace. (Num. 6:25-26)

For unto us a child is born, unto us a Son is given, and the government shall be upon His shoulder: and His name shall be called Wonderful, Counselor, The Mighty God, The Everlasting Father, The Prince of Peace. (Is. 9:6)

Finally, brethren, farewell. Be restored, be of good comfort, be of one mind, live in peace; and the God of love and peace shall be with you. (2 Cor. 13:11)

Which scripture speaks to you the most and why?

____

____

____

____

____

____

A Daily Challenge for You

We get so comfortable in our own lives that, sometimes, we even convince ourselves that we do not need to spend time with God to get peace. However, the reality is that He is the author and finisher of our faith. He is the only One that can give us the strength, wisdom, and peace we need to make it through our day. He is our peace. He is our joy. And we can only live the joyous life that He has ordained if our spirit man is poured into on a daily basis through prayer and spending time in His word! So, pick a spot in your home this week, and a time of day when you can really spend time with God and let Him pour out peace that surpasses all understanding (Philippians 4:7).

I will make sure I live in peace every day by…

This, I profess in Jesus' name!

Daily Profession of the Word of God Transformed My Life This Week By...

Look to God

You are the only one that can fulfill what God called you to do. You cannot look to man to help you with the vision God has given you as if it is dependent upon their contribution. You have to put your faith and trust in God! If you look to Him first, He will give you the direction, the instruction, and the wisdom you need to carry out His plan. He will lead you, step-by-step, in the way that you should go, and show you the people that will be an instrumental part of what He has designed. Remember, God is the one to lay the foundation. He should be the rock you stand upon which you build your business, your career, and, most importantly, your life. For in Matthew 16:18 Jesus said, *"And I say also unto thee, That thou art Peter, and upon this rock I will build my church; and the gates of hell shall not prevail against it."* In other words, Jesus was making it clear that I am not building the church or completing the assignment that God has called me to do upon anything or anyone else, but the rock of God. He is your foundation, and if you establish what you do and how you do it upon His word, then the gates of hell will not prevail against it because nothing can stand against God! So, lift your eyes to the hills from which comes your help (Psalm 121:1) and depend upon Him. He will see you through!

Daily Profess God's Word and *Look to God*

I will lift up my eyes unto the hills, from which comes my help. (Ps. 121:1)

My help comes from the Lord, who made heaven and earth. (Ps. 121:2)

The Lord is the portion of my inheritance and of my cup: you maintain my lot. (Ps. 16:5)

I would have fainted, unless I had believed to see the goodness of the Lord in the land of the living. (Ps. 27:13)

My flesh and my heart fails: but God is the strength of my heart, and my portion forever. (Ps. 73:26)

The Lord is my strength and my shield; my heart trusted in Him, and I am helped: therefore my heart greatly rejoices; and with my song will I praise Him. (Ps. 28:7)

For you are my rock and my fortress; therefore for your name's sake lead me, and guide me. (Ps. 31:3)

I will love thee, O LORD, my strength. (Ps. 18:1)

The Lord lives; and blessed be my rock; and let the God of my salvation be exalted. (Ps. 18:46)

And the Lord said, Behold, there is a place by me, and you shall stand upon a rock: (Exod. 33:21)

Which scripture speaks to you the most and why?

____

____

____

____

____

A Daily Challenge for You

There is nobody like our God! No one can match Him, supersede Him, or even come close to His omnipotence. So, why look anywhere else? So, often we look in every other direction horizontally before we look up to God. Let your look *up* be your first one this week, and watch God show you the what, how, and even give you understanding on the why!

When I look to God, He shows me…

This, I profess in Jesus' name!

Daily Profession of the Word of God Transformed My Life This Week By…

Lord, Crucify My Flesh

Sometimes, when things are going wrong, and you are consumed with ungodly thoughts and negative behaviors, you have got to say, "Lord, crucify my flesh!" Crucify my bad habits, my ungodly thoughts, my negative ways, and anything that is not like you! I am wrong. I am overwhelmed by this situation, and I realize that "I" am in the way of you resolving this matter, so, please, crucify the sin in me.

You've got to say, "Take away everything, Lord, that is hindering me and forgive me for letting this sin proliferate in my life." Galatians 5:24 says, *"And they that are Christ's have crucified the flesh with the affections and lusts."* And there is no other way you can do that and move forward, unless you cry out to God, confess your sin, repent of it, and start professing His word to help deliver you from it. Psalm 88:1-2 says, *"O Lord, God of my salvation; I cry out day and night before you. Let my prayer come before you; incline your ear to my cry."* The author knew that He could cry out to God, and God would help him. Know that God hears you; he will crucify your flesh, and help you overcome it in Jesus's name!

Daily Profess God's Word, *"Lord, Crucify My Flesh"*

O Lord, God of my salvation; I cry out day and night before you. Let my prayer come before you; incline your ear to my cry. (Ps. 88:1-2)

God is our refuge and strength, a very present help in trouble. (Ps. 46:1)

God is in the midst of her; she shall not be moved: God will help her, and that right early. (Ps. 46:5)

Then said Jesus unto His disciples, If any man will come after me, let him deny himself, and take up his cross and follow me. (Matt. 16:24)

Knowing this, that our old man is crucified with him, that the body of sin might be destroyed, that we should no longer serve sin. (Rom. 6:6)

That you put off concerning the former way of conversation the old man, which is corrupt according to the deceitful lusts. (Eph. 4:22)

Mortify therefore your members which are upon the earth; fornication, uncleanness, inordinate affection, evil desire, and covetousness, which his idolatry. (Col. 3:5)

And they that are Christ's have crucified the flesh with the affections and lusts. (Gal. 5:24)

If we confess our sins, He is faithful and just to forgive us our sins, and to cleanse us from all unrighteousness. (1 Jn 1:9)

I am crucified with Christ, nevertheless I live; yet not I, but Christ lives in me; and the life which I now live in the flesh I live by the faith of the Son of God who loved me and gave himself for me. (Gal. 2:20)

Which scripture speaks to you the most and why?

____

____

____

____

____

A Daily Challenge for You

It does not pay to continue in sin. I have been there and know what it feels like to carry the burden of bondage when I know I needed to let it go. You cannot do it by yourself, and some things only come out by prayer and fasting (Mark 9:29). However, God will see you through it and give you the power through Jesus's name to overcome it. You just have to be honest with Him, give it to Him, and let Him teach you how to live without it.

Lord, crucify my…

This, I profess in Jesus' name!

Daily Profession of the Word of God Transformed My Life This Week By…

Lord, Fill Me Up

I was running outside one day because I needed to exercise, but I also needed time with God. I just had to get outside, in the fresh air, and breathe. Breathe from the pressures of life, breathe from the pressures in my head, and breathe for me. I was consumed with thoughts and details, comings and goings, and although I had a great day doing some of things I love, I still felt empty. Now, this was interesting because at times during the day, I had complete peace and joy, and enjoyed my day off immensely. However, I still felt like I was lacking complete peace or fullness of joy. I needed something more. I needed to be filled. I needed His presence! See, there are many things in life that can make us laugh, or even give us peace of mind for a moment, but you have to ask, What is filling me? You can hang out with your best friend, or even go take a quiet walk on the beach, or a leisurely stroll in the neighborhood, but what is sustaining you?

It was at that moment, when I was outside, running in the cool of the evening, that I found the answer to that question. I needed God! I began to sing a song that talks about how he is the air I breathe and He is my daily bread. I needed to hear from God. Isaiah 55:6 says, *"Seek ye the Lord while He may be found, call upon Him while He is near."* This means God is always here for us and we just have to reach out to Him so we can be filled. So, let Him fill you with His word! As His creation, we need His Spirit, His Holy presence to fill us up and sustain us!

Daily Profess God's Word, *"Lord, Fill Me Up"*

Seek ye the Lord while He may be found, call upon Him while He is near. (Is. 55:6)

And He said, My presence shall go with you, and I will give you rest. (Exod. 33:14)

And you shall seek me, and find me, when you shall search for me with all your heart. (Jer. 29:13)

Repent ye therefore, and be converted, that your sins may be blotted out, when the times of refreshing shall come from the presence of the Lord; and He shall send Jesus Christ. Who before was preached unto you. (Acts 3:19-20)

One thing I desired of the Lord, that will I seek after; that I may dwell in the house of the Lord all he days of my life, to behold the beauty of the Lord, and to inquire in His temple. (Ps. 27:4)

But it is good for me to draw near to God: I have put my trust in the Lord God, that I may declare all your works. (Ps. 73:28)

You shall hide them in the secret of your presence form the pride of man: you shall keep them secretly in a pavilion from the strife of tongues. (Ps. 31:20)

The Lord your God in the midst of you is mighty; He will save, He will rejoice over you with joy; He will quiet you with His love, He will rejoice over you with singing. (Zeph. 3:17)

And we have known and believed the love that God has for us. God is love; and he that dwells in love dwells in God, and God in him. (1 Jn 4:16)

Glory and honor are in His presence; strength and gladness are in His place. (1 Chron. 16:27)

Which scripture speaks to you the most and why?

____

____

____

____

____

A Daily Challenge for You

Just like a car needs fuel to run, and a balloon needs air to fly, you need the presence of God in your life. It is like wind beneath your wings that doesn't just keep you afloat, but keeps you high above your circumstances and troubles that may come your way, so you can soar in life with only the peace He can give. So whether He speaks to you through His word, in prayer, or even if you feel His spirit through a song that glorifies Him, He is always ready to fill you up and give you the strength you need each day. For John 15:5 says, "*I am the vine, you are the branches: he that abides in me, and I in him, the same brings forth much fruit: for without me you can do nothing.*" Make sure to spend time in His presence each day so that God can fill you and overflow you!

Lord, fill me up with your…

This, I profess in Jesus' name!

Daily Profession of the Word of God Transformed My Life This Week By…

My Relationship with God

Our relationship with God is everything! It is where we find our joy, our peace, our drive to move forward and be who God has called us to be. And I love the relationship we can have with Him because He is right there for us, looking out for our every need, and blessing us with the desires of our heart as we faithfully serve Him. He is so precious, caring, loving, kind, thoughtful, and yet so strong, protective, a warrior who will fight our battles for us! What can beat that? It makes my heart smile just thinking of how much God covers us and nurtures us, paying attention to every detail about us that He intricately designed for His glory and our destiny. I love Him so much that it hurts. I could not imagine life without Him! The fact that He loves us no matter what we have done, and His love is so unconditional, just blows my mind. It is bananas! David says it best in Psalm 139:7-10, *"Where shall I go from your spirit? Or where shall I flee from thy presence? If I ascend up into heaven, you are there: if I make my bed in hell, behold, you are there. If I take the wings of the morning, and dwell in the uttermost parts of the sea; Even there shall your hand lead me, and your right hand shall hold me."*

Just know that you are loved beyond what you can imagine, and God is always with you! He cares for you and created you to be His own. Don't ever forget that.

Daily Profess God's Word for "*My Relationship with God*"

Where shall I go from your spirit? Or where shall I flee from thy presence? If I ascend up into heaven, you are there: if I make my bed in hell, behold, you are there. If I take the wings of the morning, and dwell in the uttermost parts of the sea; Even there shall your hand lead me, and your right hand shall hold me. (Ps. 139:7-10).

For I know the thoughts that I think toward you, says the Lord, thoughts of peace, and not evil, to give you an expected end. (Jer. 29:11)

But as many as received Him, to them gave he power to become the children of God, even to them that believe on his name. Who were born, not of blood, nor of the will of the flesh, nor of the will of man, but of God. (Jn 1:12-13)

Jesus said unto him, I am the way, the truth, and the life: no man comes unto the Father, but by me. (Jn 14:6)

But God commends His love toward us, in that, while we were yet sinners, Christ died for us. (Rom. 5:8)

If we confess our sins, He is faithful and just to forgive us our sins, and to cleanse us from all unrighteousness. (1 Jn 1:9)

And this is the will of Him that sent me, that everyone who sees the Son, and believes on Him, may have everlasting life: and I will raise Him up at the last day. (Jn 6:40)

Neither I pray for these alone, but for them also which shall believe on me through their word. That they all may be one; as you, Father, are in me, and I in you, that they also may be one in us: that the world may believe that you have sent me. (Jn 17:20-21)

But without faith it is impossible to please him: for he that comes to God must believe that He is, and that He is a rewarder of them that diligently seek Him. (Heb. 11:6)

Behold, I stand at the door, and knock: if any man hears my voice, and opens the door, I will come in to him, and will eat with him, and he with me. (Rev. 3:20)

Which scripture speaks to you the most and why?

____

____

____

____

____

____

____

A Daily Challenge for You

God already loves us beyond measure. It is now our turn to embrace Him! We need to cherish our relationship with God more now than ever before. Because at the end of the day, He is the one who gives us the provision to put clothes on our back and food on our table, as the old saints used to say. And He is the only one we can call on and who will be there at any time, any place, anywhere. So, take care of your relationship with God by putting Him first each day. Say "Good morning, Holy Spirit, you are welcome in this place," as soon as you get up and spend time hearing what He has to say through His word so that you can strengthen your relationship with Him!

My relationship with God was strengthened today because…

This, I profess in Jesus' name!

Daily Profession of the Word of God Transformed My Life This Week By…

Never Again

In a day and time like today, it is the perfect season to say, "Never again." There are so many things going on in our world, from the war against terrorism, racism, violence, abuse, arguments over sexual preference, to even horrific weather storms that are topping the charts. It can cause one to be wrapped up in an emotional whirlwind of times and people that are changing every day. However, God quickened me the other day and said, "You do not have to live based upon what the world does or what man says or thinks. You just have to live by what my Word says, and by what I have established through it."

I realized at that moment that God created the heavens and the earth, and I am a part of what He created. Therefore, I never have to be overwhelmed, discouraged, or look to man for stability because God has not changed. Malachi 3:6 says, *"For I am the Lord, I change not; therefore, you sons of Jacob are not consumed."*

So, I have to declare that never again do I have to worry, or doubt, or fret when I can lean on the very *one* who is in control in the first place. He is the one who created me, established me, and has great plans for me, my family, my children, and for His people. I have just got to keep my eyes on Him, rest in His sovereignty, and say to fear, doubt, distress, and despair, "Never again." Then I can rest in His joy, His peace, and His protection. I can let Him lead me because He is God, and I belong to Him!

Daily Profess God's Word for "*Never Again*"

> For I am the Lord, I change not; therefore, you sons of Jacob are not consumed. (Mal. 3:6)
>
> But Jesus beheld [them], and said unto them, with men this is impossible; but with God all things are possible. (Matt. 19:26)
>
> Then spake Jesus again unto them, saying, I am the light of the world: he that followeth me shall not walk in darkness, but shall have the light of life. (Jn 8:12)
>
> And your ears shall hear a word behind you, saying, This is the way, walk you in it, when you turn to the right hand, and when you turn to the left. (Is. 30:21)
>
> I will lead the blind by ways they have not known, along unfamiliar paths I will guide them; I will turn the darkness into light before them and make the rough places smooth. These are the things I will do; I will not forsake them. (Is. 42:16)

> He guides the humble in what is right and teaches them his way. (Ps. 25:9)
>
> In all your ways submit to him, and he will make your paths straight. (Prov. 3:6)
>
> This is what the Lord says—your Redeemer, the Holy One of Israel: "I am the Lord your God, who teaches you what is best for you, who directs you in the way you should go. (Is. 48:17)

Which scripture speaks to you the most and why?

____

____

____

____

____

A Daily Challenge for You

My challenge to you is to not live your life in fear of what goes on in our world or be consumed by the ever-changing times. You've got to live based upon what God has ordained for you and according to His plan for your life. This means that every day, you must get His wisdom and His direction from His word, so that you can have His joy and live in His peace in all that you do. So, start your day with Him, profess His word, and stand upon it no matter what. Say "Never again," to worry, doubt, or fear!

Never again will I…

____

____

____

____

____

____

____

____

____

____

____

____

This, I profess in Jesus' name!

Daily Profession of the Word of God Transformed My Life This Week By…

New Life

There is always a new level and a new life for you! It is a new place and time in your life to do something you haven't done and to accomplish what you have yet to achieve. It is an opportunity to leave the past behind and grab hold of your future, your God-given destiny. So, don't let anyone or anything stop you—not even yourself! I had to say this to myself the other day. I had to say I can write my blog, work on my second book, and most of all, love and serve the Lord my God with all my heart! I can still be the best wife and mom I could ever be and enjoy time with my family! I can have peace in Christ in the midst of my full, busy, and sometimes hectic days, and still expect the impossible that only God can do!

In reality, I had to crucify my flesh, my own ways, and my own fears of not balancing it all that I had become so comfortable with. I had to ask God to baptize me in mind, soul, and spirit and teach me how to live on this new level in my life that He has brought me to. And this is what God said to me that I want to share with you! Romans 6:4 says, *"Therefore we are buried with Him in baptism into death: that like as Christ was raised up from the dead by the glory of God the Father; even so we also should walk in newness of life."*

God wants you to have *newness* of life in Him! Jesus died and rose again just for you to experience the new life in Him that He has given you! So, embrace the deliverance He has already promised you from your past, and let God be your guide to fulfill all He has ordained you to do! Go forth this year and live for Him! This I profess for you in Jesus's name!

Daily Profess God's Word for *New Life*

Therefore, we are buried with Him in baptism into death: that like as Christ was raised up from the dead by the glory of God the Father; even so we also should walk in newness of life. (Rom. 6:4)

Jesus said, "The thief does not come except to steal, and to kill, and to destroy. I have come that they may have life, and that they may have *it* more abundantly." (Jn 10:10)

That you put off, concerning your former conduct, the old man which grows corrupt according to the deceitful lusts, and be renewed in the spirit of your mind, and that you put on the new man which was created according to God, in true righteousness and holiness. (Eph. 4:22-24)

Most assuredly, I say to you, he who hears My word and believes in Him who sent Me has everlasting life, and shall not come into judgment, but has passed from death into life. (Jn 5:24)

Then He who sat on the throne said, "Behold, I make all things new." And He said to me, "Write, for these words are true and faithful." (Rev. 21:5)

Therefore, if anyone *is* in Christ, *he is* a new creation; old things have passed away; behold, all things have become new. (2 Cor. 5:17)

Behold, I will do a new thing, now it shall spring forth; shall you not know it? I will even make a road in the wilderness a*nd* rivers in the desert. (Is. 43:19)

Which scripture speaks to you the most and why?

____

____

____

____

____

____

A Daily Challenge for You

There is nothing like the smell of something *new*, fresh, and exciting in your life! God has so many things that He wants to do for you this year. It is more than just a New Year's resolution. It is what He has *promised* for you! So, erase the past. You cannot change it anyway. Look forward to what is *new* and ask God to help you step by step and day by day to live the *new life* He has given you! Believe Him and receive it today!

The new life you have given me is…

____

____

____

____

____

____

____

____

____

____

This, I profess in Jesus' name!

Daily Profession of the Word of God Transformed My Life This Week By…

Our Worship to God Is Everything!

Our worship unto God is everything! It reminds us of His power. It reminds us of His grace. It reminds us of His love for us, and that He will never leave us alone. We need our time of worship with Him. We need to experience His presence on a daily basis, wherever we go. There are so many things that can hinder us from feeling protected, peaceful, covered, or safe; tragic happenings, discord, and confusion that can make us feel as if we are on our own. But God is in control. He is right there, every day, waiting to direct us, comfort us, pour into us with His word, so that we can experience daily just how real He is! David said it best: *"I would have fainted, unless I had believed to see the goodness of the Lord in the land of the living"* (Ps. 27:13). So, be encouraged today. Despite everything going in your life or in this world, know that He is with you, protecting you, keeping you, and carrying you through. Run to Him and spend time in His arms, in prayer, or even in song. He is your LORD, your Savior, your matchless king. You are His child, His creation, for whom He will do anything!

Daily Profess God's Word for *"Our Worship to God Is Everything!"*

I would have fainted, unless I had believed to see the goodness of the LORD in the land of the living. (Ps. 27:13)

Then saith Jesus unto him, Get thee hence, Satan: for it is written, Thou shalt worship the Lord thy God, and him only shalt thou serve. (Matt. 4:10)

And you shall serve the LORD your God, and he shall bless your bread, and your water; and I will take sickness away from the midst of you. There shall nothing miscarry, nor be barren, in your land: the number of your days I will fulfill. (Exod. 23:25-26)

For thou shalt worship no other god: for the LORD, whose name *is* Jealous, *is* a jealous God (Exod. 34:14)

Give unto the LORD the glory due unto His name; bring an offering, and come before Him; worship the LORD in the beauty of holiness. (1 Chron. 16:29)

But as for me, I will come into Thy house in the multitude of Thy mercy, and in Thy fear will I worship toward Thy holy temple. (Ps. 5:7)

O come, let us worship and bow down; let us kneel before the LORD our Maker. (Ps. 95:6)

But the hour cometh and now is, when the true worshipers shall worship the Father in spirit and in truth; for the Father seeketh such to worship Him. God is a Spirit, and they that worship Him must worship Him in spirit and in truth. (Jn 4:23-24)

All nations whom Thou hast made shall come and worship before thee, O Lord, and shall glorify Thy name. (Ps. 86:9)

Which scripture speaks to you the most and why?

____

____

____

____

____

A Daily Challenge for You

We have to give our all unto Him because He gave it unto us. If you sit still long enough, you know that there is the one and only God who made you, watches over you, and takes care of you that you need to get know more every day. It is in His presence that we find joy, peace, strength, wisdom, and direction.

So just try this week to find the time, whether it be a few minutes or an hour, to just sit still before Him and let Him speak to you. Then take it a step further and serve Him based upon what you received of Him. Let Him fill you. Let His loving arms surround you. Let Him lead you. I promise, you will feel the difference in your mind, body, soul, and spirit, and you will be more a light to someone else along the way!

I will worship you by…

____

____

____

____

____

____

____

____

____

This, I profess in Jesus' name!

Daily Profession of the Word of God Transformed My Life This Week By...

Pray in the Midst of the Attack

Have you ever been under spiritual warfare that is so high that you can't even call it by name? Attacks may be coming every direction, on your job, tension in relationships, problems at home, even turmoil with your children, and you haven't really had the space and time to deal with it. It is time to shout *attack* in your spirit, and ask the angels God has given you to fight the battle for you. There is a time at midnight, which, according to the Bible is the highest time of spiritual warfare where the enemy seeks to wreak havoc spiritually. This is the time when most people are sleeping and not even thinking that they need to pray. However, this is also a time when miraculous breakthroughs happen when you pray against those demonic forces that seek to steal, kill, and destroy (John 10:10). Like in Acts 16:25-34, when Paul and Silas were thrown in jail by the magistrates of the city for delivering a damsel who was demon possessed. However, at midnight, when Paul and Silas prayed and sang praises unto God, there was a great earthquake and the foundations of the prison were shaken, doors were opened, and everyone's bands were loosed!

See, God wants you to know today that despite how great the attack that is coming against you, He will fight the battle for you if you take the time to *pray* and give God *praise* even in the midst of it! He wants you to know that He will come and see about you when you trust Him, put Him first, and above your situation. Just know that when you do, God will get the glory, lives will be delivered, and people will come to know Jesus by your testimony; just like the jailer who got saved because of Paul's and Silas's faith. God loves you, and He is waiting to deliver you from *all* your fears (Psalm 34:4) so shout *attack* in Jesus's name and watch Him move on your behalf. This I profess in Jesus's name!

Daily Profess God's Word and *Pray in the Midst of the Attack*

The thief does not come except to steal, and to kill, and to destroy. I have come that they may have life, and that they may have *it* more abundantly. (Jn 10:10)

I sought the Lord, and He heard me, and delivered me from all my fears. (Ps. 34:4)

But at midnight Paul and Silas were praying and singing hymns to God, and the prisoners were listening to them. Suddenly there was a great earthquake, so that the foundations of the prison were shaken; and immediately all the doors were opened and everyone's chains were loosed. (Acts 16:25-27)

Then they cry out to the LORD in their trouble, and He brings them out of their distresses. He calms the storm, so that its waves are still. Then they are glad because they are quiet; so He guides them to their desired haven. (Ps. 107:28-30)

And he said to them, "This kind cannot be driven out by anything but prayer." (Mk 9:29)

Whatever you ask in my name, this I will do, that the Father may be glorified in the Son. If you ask me anything in my name, I will do it. (Jn 14:13-14)

I will sing unto the LORD as long as I live: I will sing praise to my God while I have my being. (Ps. 104:33)

And he has put a new song in my mouth, even praise unto our God: many shall see it, and fear, and shall trust in the LORD. (Ps. 40:3)

Which scripture speaks to you the most and why?

____

____

____

____

____

____

____

____

____

A Daily Challenge for You

If there is any type of spiritual warfare, negative things that are happening in your life, I challenge you to *pray* when God leads you to. It may be at midnight or another time of the day, but whenever God leads you to pray this week, *pray*. Sing songs unto the Lord and rejoice in the fact that you have the victory over the enemy or any warfare that is coming against you, because of the resurrection power of Jesus Christ in your life. Matthew 21:22 says, *"And whatever you ask in prayer, you will receive, if you have faith."*

I will sing unto the Lord and pray that…

This, I profess in Jesus' name!

Daily Profession of the Word of God Transformed My Life This Week By...

Put God First and Jump All the Way In!

You have to ask yourself some honest-to-God questions about what you put first in your life and what you deem as valuable. Most people will say my family, my relationship with God, my career goals and accomplishments, my church, and the ministry I serve in. But what are you most passionate about? And is it a hobby or is it a part of your destiny?

I realized when I was watching the show called *Shark Tank* that if you really value something or have a passion for something, and it is a part of the very fiber of your being, you are willing to take a risk for it. However, if it is just a hobby you enjoy, but you don't have to do it every day, you will not give up everything for it.

So, with that analogy, how do you feel about your relationship with God and the ministry you serve in? Is it just a hobby that you enjoy but you're not willing to give up much for it, *or* is it a part of your destiny, and you are willing to take the risk of putting Him first before anything else? For taking risks and giving your all can be scary, and you can receive a lot of flak for doing so from those who are only willing to stay in their comfort zone. On the other hand, the reward in Christ that you receive is *greater* than you could ever imagine, and He alone will get the glory and honor you for your commitment to Him! Psalm 50:14-15 says, *"Offer unto God thanksgiving; and pay your vows unto the most High: And call on me in the day of trouble: I will deliver you, and you shall glorify me."* He is waiting for you to take that risk, that proverbial "step of faith" and trust Him. Just put God first and give Him all you have. Jump all the way into what He has given you a passion to do and serve Him. For He will take care of the rest and cover you with His protection and glory as you go further into your destiny! This I profess in Jesus's name!

Daily Profess God's Word and *Put God First*

> Offer unto God thanksgiving; and pay your vows unto the most High: And call on me in the day of trouble: I will deliver you, and you shall glorify me. (Ps. 50:14-15)
>
> But seek ye first the kingdom of God, and his righteousness; and all these things shall be added unto you. (Matt. 6:33)
>
> If ye then be risen with Christ, seek those things which are above, where Christ sitteth on the right hand of God. (Col. 3:1)

For they that are after the flesh do mind the things of the flesh; but they that are after the Spirit the things of the Spirit. (Rom. 8:5)

Jesus said unto him, Thou shalt love the Lord thy God with all thy heart, and with all thy soul, and with all thy mind. (Matt. 22:37)

I am the vine, ye [are] the branches: He that abideth in me, and I in him, the same bringeth forth much fruit: for without me ye can do nothing. (Jn 15:5)

So will I sing praise unto thy name for ever, that I may daily perform my vows. (Ps. 61:8)

Thou shalt make thy prayer unto him, and he shall hear thee, and thou shalt pay thy vows. (Job 22:27)

Whether therefore ye eat, or drink, or whatsoever ye do, do all to the glory of God. (2 Cor. 10:31)

Which scripture speaks to you the most and why?

____

____

____

____

____

____

____

A Daily Challenge for You

We give our all to a lot of things. We give our all to our children, to our favorite pastimes, and, most of all, we give our all to what we love. However, if God is truly the center of your joy and the Savior of your life, you have to examine if you are giving your all to Him by putting Him first each day. This is a daily challenge that we have to be willing to do. So the next time you wake up in the morning, try putting Him first. Put Him first in your mind, your actions, and your deeds by giving Him praise, reading His word, and seeking to follow His lead before you even start your day.

I will put God first by…

This, I profess in Jesus' name!

Daily Profession of the Word of God Transformed My Life This Week By...

Raise Your Level of Expectation Even More!

It is time to raise our expectation level even more! I have learned this week to expect what only God can do; not man, not money, not Mama, or what your job can provide, just God! There is a realm that God operates in that is completely different then the world that we live in each day. He is the Creator, the Alpha and the Omega, the beginning and the end. Therefore, He can see the whole spectrum of time. He is omniscient, all-knowing, and He sees beyond what we see! He knows what direction we should take. He knows what decisions we should make! So, in the midst of such troubled times and circumstances we sometimes don't understand, we need to seek His face and hear clearly through His Word, what we *may* have overlooked before!

We've got to *expect healing*, for by His stripes you are healed (1 Peter 2:24). Expect deliverance, for Psalm 34:4 says, *"I sought the Lord, and he heard me, and delivered me from all my fears."* Expect greater, for He said in Ephesians 3:20 *"Now unto Him who is able to do exceedingly, abundantly above all you ask or think according to the power that works in us!"* Expect God, for He is Jehovah Jireh, our provider (Genesis 22:14)! He is Jehovah Shammah, The Lord is there (Ezekiel 48:35)! He is Jehovah Nissi, the Lord is our banner, which means we have the victory over anything the enemy tries to send because God will fight the battle for His people (Exodus 17:15)! He is Jehovah Tsideknu, The Lord is my righteousness, which means we are redeemed by the blood of the Lamb. He is our peace, our way maker, and there is no one like Him. We must raise our level of *expectation* for it only should come from Him (Psalm 62:5). So, put your trust in Him, watch God move, and He will transform your life! This I profess in Jesus name!

Daily Profess God's Word and *Raise Your Level of Expectation Even More!*

> I sought the Lord, and he heard me, and delivered me from all my fears. (Ps. 34:4)
>
> Now unto Him who is able to do exceedingly, abundantly above all you ask or think according to the power that works in us. (Eph. 3:20)
>
> And Abraham called the name of the place, The-Lord-Will-Provide; as it said *to* this day, "In the Mount of the Lord it shall be provided." (Gen. 22:14)

My soul, wait silently for God alone, For my expectation *is* from Him. (Ps. 62:5)

Then the LORD said to Moses, "Write this *for* a memorial in the book and recount *it* in the hearing of Joshua, that I will utterly blot out the remembrance of Amalek from under heaven." And Moses built an altar and called its name, The-LORD-Is-My-Banner. (Exod. 17:14-15)

O Lord God, You have begun to show Your servant Your greatness and Your mighty hand, for what god *is there* in heaven or on earth who can do *anything* like Your works and Your mighty deeds? (Deut. 3:24)

God *is* not a man, that He should lie, nor a son of man, that He should repent. Has He said, and will He not do? Or has He spoken, and will He not make it good? (Num. 23:19)

Which scripture speaks to you the most and why?

____

____

____

____

____

____

____

____

A Daily Challenge for You

Your level of expectation is determined by your faith in God. Whatever you are believing God to do in your life, you have to begin to trust Him just for who He is. So, this week, write down and declare the attributes of God and find a few scriptures that go with it. Declare His name against any situation that arises and profess His word no matter how it looks or how it feels. God will be faithful to show Himself strong, and you will be glad that you raised your expectation of Him because you know the power of His name!

I raise my expectation level even more by declaring that God is…

____

____

____

____

____

____

____

____

____

____

____

____

____

____

____

This, I profess in Jesus' name!

Daily Profession of the Word of God Transformed My Life This Week By...

Refuge in God

There is something to be said for those who stay faithful to the call of God in their lives, despite what anyone else says, does, or thinks. There is a resolve that only a true believer can have that will stand in the midst of adversity, peril, trial, or stress and literally hide and take refuge in the presence of the Lord, like a young son would hide under the arm of His father when they are scared. There is a protection and a safety in the master's arm that no man can replace, that no relationship can supersede. No one is that important to take over your relationship with God or to outweigh it. There is a place in God that no man or devil in hell can touch. For Psalm 91:1-2 says, *"He that dwells in the secret place of the most high shall abide under the shadow of the almighty. I will say of the Lord, He is my refuge and my fortress: my God; in Him will I trust."* No one can touch that because God made the heavens and earth. He is the giver of life and He can take it away. He will be there for you when no one else will and the very thing or person that is trying to challenge that in your life will not.

So, all you need to do is hide in His presence, seek His face, and hold on to His word like it is your very breath. There is power in your profession of His promises, knowing that God will see you through that situation or level of attack that is coming your way. *"For God is not a man that he should lie, neither the son of man that he should repent: has He said, and shall he not do it? Or has He spoken, and shall he not make it good?"* (Num. 23:19). When all else fails and even when everything is okay, do not dare look to man to be your source of whatever you need or desire. Just take refuge in God and let Him take you to a place of protection, peace, deliverance, and strength that you have never known. Let Him show you what it is really like to have a relationship with Him and to be covered by His love! This I profess in Jesus's name.

Daily Profess God's Word for *Refuge in God*

> He that dwells in the secret place of the most high shall abide under the shadow of the almighty. I will say of the LORD, He is my refuge and my fortress: my God; in Him will I trust. (Ps. 91:1-2)
>
> God is not a man that he should lie, neither the son of man that he should repent: has He said, and shall he not do it? Or has He spoken, and shall he not make it good? (Num. 23:19)
>
> The LORD is my rock, and my fortress, and my deliverer; my God, my strength, in whom I trust;

my shield, and the horn of my salvation, and my high tower. (Ps. 18:2)

The Lord is my strength and song, and He is become my salvation: He is my God, and I will prepare Him a habitation; my father's God, and I will exalt Him. (Exod. 15:2)

O my God, I trust in you: let me not be ashamed, let not my enemies triumph over me. (Ps. 25:2)

I cried unto you, O Lord; I said, Thou art my hope and my portion in the land of the living. (Ps. 142:5)

But the Lord is my defense; and my God is the rock of my refuge. (Ps. 94:22)

I am as a wonder unto many: but you are my strong refuge. (Ps. 71:7)

You are my hiding place; you shall preserve me from trouble; thou shalt compass me about with songs of deliverance. (Ps. 32:7)

You are my hiding place and my shield: I hope in your word. (Ps. 119:114)

Which scripture speaks to you the most and why?

____

____

____

____

____

____

____

My Daily Challenge to You

It is very easy to freak out in any situation or circumstance and feel like you have nowhere to run. However, when you have a real relationship with God, you will realize that He is right there for you, waiting to embrace you with His love and promises that will help you make it through. His word is true, and He promised to take care of you. So my challenge to you is to *run* to Him and stay in His presence and watch Him protect your mind, guard your heart, strengthen your body, and pour into your soul through His word. Let Him carry you and bring you through stronger than you were before.

I will take refuge in God by…

This, I profess in Jesus' name!

Daily Profession of the Word of God Transformed My Life This Week By...

Shine Bright

At noon, the sun is at its highest. It is shining bright and at its fullest. It is at this time that we can be reminded that we should live our lives bright so that God will get the glory out of what we do! This is also the time of the day to rest, where we pray against the destruction at noonday (Psalm 91:6) and know that God will fulfill His promises. For Psalm 91:1 says, *"He who dwells in the secret place of the Most High shall abide under the shadow of the Almighty. I will say of the Lord, "He is my refuge and my fortress; My God, in Him will I trust."* We can rest in the fact that He is covering us, protecting us, and taking care of us as His own. We can rejoice in the fact that He has designed us, given us purpose, and will make sure that what He has begun in us, He will complete (Philippians 1:6). So then, we can marvel at the fact that *"because He has set His love upon Me, therefore I will deliver Him; I will set him on high, because He has known My name"* (Psalm 91:14). In other words, we can be glad that He has called us out of darkness into the marvelous light, so that we can shine bright and live our lives completely for Him. For God says it best in Matthew 5:14-16 *"You are the light of the world. A city that is set on a hill cannot be hid. Nor do they light a lamp and put it under a basket, but on a lampstand, and it gives light to all who are in the house. Let your light so shine before men, that they may see your good works and glorify your Father in Heaven."* This I profess in Jesus's name!

Daily Profess God's Word and *Shine Bright*

He who dwells in the secret place of the Most High shall abide under the shadow of the Almighty. I will say of the Lord, "He is my refuge and my fortress; My God, in Him will I trust. (Ps. 91:1)

Because He has set His love upon Me, therefore I will deliver Him; I will set him on high, because He has known My name. (Ps. 91:14)

But if we walk in the light, as he is in the light, we have fellowship one with another, and the blood of Jesus Christ his Son cleanseth us from all sin. (1 Jn 1:7)

And behold, the glory of the God of Israel was coming from the way of the east and His voice was like the sound of many waters; and the earth shone with His glory. (Ezekiel 43:2)

The Lord make His face shine on you, and be gracious to you. (Num. 6:25)

For God, who commanded the light to shine out of darkness, hath shined in our hearts, to [give] the light of the knowledge of the glory of God in the face of Jesus Christ. (2 Cor. 4:6)

Those who are wise shall shine like the brightness of the firmament, and those who turn many to righteousness like the stars forever and ever. (Dan. 12:3)

You are the light of the world. A city that is set on a hill cannot be hid. Nor do they light a lamp and put it under a basket, but on a lampstand, and it gives light to all who are in the house. Let your light so shine before men, that they may see your good works and glorify your Father in Heaven. (Matt. 5:14-16)

Then spake Jesus again unto them, saying, I am the light of the world: he that followeth me shall not walk in darkness, but shall have the light of life. (Jn 8:12)

Then the righteous will shine forth as the sun in the kingdom of their Father. He who has ears to hear, let him hear! (Matt. 13:43)

Which scripture speaks to you the most and why?

____

____

____

____

____

____

____

____

A Daily Challenge for You

You know the plans that God has for you to be a shining light in this world. So shine bright! Show His love in some way to those around you and be a witness for Him. Whether it be giving a smile to someone in the store, helping someone in need, or making an encouraging phone call to someone in your family out of the blue, and let God's light shine through you. Laugh, love, live, and don't worry about what comes against you. Watch Him get the glory from you living a life that pleases Him!

I will shine bright by…

This, I profess in Jesus' name!

Daily Profession of the Word of God Transformed My Life This Week By…

Step-by-Step, Go Forth!

Have you been making plans for this year? I mean, really… have you been writing down things that you want to do? Setting goals? Strategically planning how you're going to accomplish it? If you haven't already done so, you need to do so now, because if you don't, you never will! Time is of the essence. There are things that God wants to do in you right now. You have heard his voice and know in your heart what you are supposed to do. So, seek His direction and receive His instruction on what to do first. Ephesians 5:15-17 says, *"Look carefully then how you walk, not as unwise but as wise, making the best use of the time, because the days are evil. Therefore, do not be foolish, but understand what the will of the Lord is."* So, take the time to do so. Every day, do something new. Little by little, step-by-step, you will meet your goal if you stay consistent, persistent, and diligent with what God has called you to do. No one can do it better than you! Believe that. I am praying for you as you go forth in Jesus's name!

Daily Profess God's Word and *Step-by-Step, Go Forth*

Look carefully then how you walk, not as unwise but as wise, making the best use of the time, because the days are evil. Therefore, do not be foolish, but understand what the will of the Lord is. (Eph. 5:15-17)

Order my steps in your word: and let not any iniquity have dominion over me. (Ps. 119:133)

Hold up my steps in your paths, that my feet slip not. (Ps. 17:5)

You have enlarged my path under me, that my feet did not slip. (Ps. 18:36)

I will instruct you and teach you in the way which you shall go: I will guide you with my eye. (Ps. 32:8)

The steps of a good man are ordered by the Lord: and he delights in his way. (Ps. 37:23)

Show me your ways, O Lord; teach me your paths. Lead me in your truth, and teach me: for you are the God of my salvation; on you do I wait all the day. (Ps. 25:4-5)

> For you shall go out with joy, and be led forth with peace: the mountains and the hills shall break forth before you into singing, and all the trees of the field shall clap their hands. (Is. 55:12)

Which scripture speaks to you the most and why?

____

____

____

____

____

My Daily Challenge to You

God knows the plans that He has for you (Jeremiah 29:11). So, as you go forth, seek His direction daily. He can tell you what you need to do day by day and step by step. You just have to make sure you put yourself in position to *hear* His voice every day. This means that your time with God is crucial. The daily bread you get from Him will help lead you to fulfill your destiny. So, this week, start the habit of writing down all the instructions God gives you and move forward in Jesus's name!

God, you are telling me step-by-step to…

This, I profess in Jesus' name!

Daily Profession of the Word of God Transformed My Life This Week By...

Take a Risk by Faith

During the middle of the July, when it is hot and muggy, we need a time of refreshing, renewal, and restoration! We need it because, sometimes, when it is hot, even in life, you can become lazy and lose motivation to want to do anything. You get lackadaisical, start to procrastinate, and your faith sometimes becomes dormant and stale because you are overcome with the heat of your circumstances.

Well, one thing that I received was this is the time in our lives when we need to revive our faith. We also must realize that it is not faith unless you take a risk in obedience to God to move in what He called you to do. In this day and time, why not? We always have dreams, desires, and things we know we should be doing, but a lot of times, they never get done because we are overwhelmed with the routine of our current day and not willing to step out on faith and do something different. Hebrews 11:6 says, *"But without faith it is impossible to please Him: for he that comes to God must believe that He is, and that He is a rewarder of him that diligently seeks Him."* So, take the risk! Step out on faith and do what God has called you to do. Hebrews 11 is full of believers who did great things *by faith*, despite the odds against them. Do what God is calling you to do by just taking one step at a time, day by day, by faith. Romans 10:17 says, *"Faith comes by hearing and hearing by the word of God."* So, let Him encourage you, "by His word," and no matter how hot it is in your life, do not be dismayed. Take the risk anyway by faith! This I profess, declare, and will do in Jesus' name!

Daily Profess God's Word and *Take a Risk by Faith*

For we walk by faith, not by sight. (2 Cor. 5:7)

What shall we then say to these things? If God be for us, who can be against us?" (Rom. 8:31)

And he that taketh not his cross, and followeth after me, is not worthy of me." (Matt. 10:38)

For therein is the righteousness of God revealed from faith to faith: as it is written, The just shall live by faith. (Rom. 1:17)

Now faith is the substance of things hoped for, the evidence of things not seen. (Heb. 11:1)

So then faith [cometh] by hearing, and hearing by the word of God. (Rom. 10:17)

Have not I commanded you? Be strong and of a good courage; be not afraid, neither be you dismayed: for the LORD your God is with you wherever you go. (Josh. 1:9)

Then said Jesus unto his disciples, If any man will come after me, let him deny himself, and take up his cross, and follow me. (Matt. 16:24)

If any of you lacks wisdom, let him ask of God, who gives to all liberally and without reproach, and it will be given to him. But let him ask in faith, with no doubting, for he who doubts is like a wave of the sea driven and tossed by the wind. For let not that man suppose that he will receive anything from the Lord; he is a double-minded man, unstable in all his ways. (Jas 1:5-8)

Which scripture speaks to you the most and why?

____

____

____

____

____

____

A Daily Challenge for You

It is time-out for excuses and taking forever to do what you know God has called you to do. He has placed it in your spirit to do it because He knows that it will be a blessing to His people and glorify His name. He has given you all the tools you need to walk out your purpose. So, take the first step *by faith* and do something *every day* that will be pleasing to God while moving forward in your destiny!

This, I profess in Jesus' name!

Daily Profession of the Word of God Transformed My Life This Week By...

The Desires of Your Heart

God wants to give us the desires of our heart, but we have to be willing to not put those desires before Him. Psalm 37:4 says, *"Delight thyself also in the Lord; and he shall give thee the desires of thine heart."* He will take care of what we dream of and care to do if we sit back, relax, and enjoy the relationship He has given us with Him. But why is that so hard for us? Because we are constantly faced every day with the challenges of being overly consumed with our day, or the temptation to be overwhelmed with stress, or even burdened down with depression or despair. It is very easy to focus on the negative or even get caught up in the rudimentary daily routine and not enjoy your relationship with Christ.

This is why we have to do a self-examination check daily. Let me share some things that God told me. Put God first. Spend time in His presence and seek His face through His Word. Do what God is calling you to do for His Kingdom and serve in ministry by getting involved in what you are passionate about for His glory, and He will show you the delight that comes from living for Him. If you seek to enjoy getting to know Him more every day and have your eyes and your mind open to what He will show you, He will bless you to live the life He has ordained you to live. For Matthew 6:33, *"Seek ye first the Kingdom of God and his righteousness and all these things will be added unto you."* And God promised that He will do just what He said.

Daily Profess God's Word for the *"Desires of Your Heart"*

Delight thyself also in the LORD; and he shall give thee the desires of thine heart. (Ps. 37:4)

Seek ye first the Kingdom of God and his righteousness and all these things will be added unto you. (Matt. 6:33)

Commit your way to the LORD, trust also in Him, and He will do it. (Ps. 37:5)

The preparations of the heart belong to man, but the answer of the tongue is, is from the LORD. All the ways of a man are clean in his own eyes; but the LORD weighs the spirits. (Prov. 16:1-2)

A man's heart plans his way: but the LORD directs his steps. (Prov. 16:9)

> Trust in the Lord with all your heart; and lean not to your own understanding. In all your ways acknowledge Him, and He shall direct your paths. (Prov. 3:5-6)

> For where you treasure is, there will your heart be also. (Matt. 6:21)

Which scripture speaks to you the most and why?

____

____

____

____

____

A Daily Challenge for You

I have not met too many people who don't want to be happy in life. At the end of the day, most of us want to enjoy the life we live and have peace living it. So my challenge to you is to spend time with God daily and to guard your heart and your mind from anything that would try and steal your peace and joy He has given you. That can only happen as you delight yourself in Him by professing His promises even when it gets hard. Just know He will bless you abundantly as you rest and find joy in Him!

I will delight in God every day by…

____

____

____

____

____

____

____

____

____

____

____

____

____

____

This, I profess in Jesus' name!

Daily Profession of the Word of God Transformed My Life This Week By...

The Road to Deliverance

There is a road to deliverance that everyone must take. It is a battle that takes place in your spirit between your new self and your old self that rages within. One part holds you back, and the other part wants to move you forward. However, you have to ask yourself, which part of me is going to win? How do you overcome? Well in that "moment" you have to call upon His word. Romans 13:14 says, *"But put ye on the Lord Jesus Christ and make not provision for the flesh, to fulfill the lusts thereof."* You have to ask Jesus for help and to do what He would do. If it is pride, call on him to humble you. If it is anger, ask Him for peace. Whatever you do, keep professing His word out of your mouth and ask him for help in Jesus's name until the old habits, traits, or ways break. Transformation will come and manifestation of His promises will take place. Just keep walking in it and professing it in Jesus's name! You will overcome! This I profess in Jesus' name, amen!

Daily Profess God's Word for *"The Road to Deliverance"*

But put ye on the Lord Jesus Christ and make not provision for the flesh, to fulfill the lusts thereof. (Rom. 13:14)

Pride *goes* before destruction, and a haughty spirit before a fall. Better *to be* of a humble spirit with the lowly, than to divide the spoil with the proud. (Prov. 16:18-19)

The righteous cry, and the Lord heareth, and delivereth them out of all their troubles. (Ps. 34:17)

And call upon me in the day of trouble: I will deliver thee, and thou shalt glorify me. (Ps. 50:15)

If ye abide in me, and my words abide in you, ye shall ask what ye will, and it shall be done unto you. (Jn 15:7)

The Lord knoweth how to deliver the godly out of temptations, and to reserve the unjust unto the day of judgment to be punished. (2 Pet. 2:9)

For sin shall not have dominion over you: for ye are not under the law, but under grace. (Rom. 6:14)

Which scripture speaks to you the most and why?

____

____

____

____

____

____

____

A Daily Challenge for You

We have a choice to make in life each day that we wake up. We can either live free or live in bondage. And it starts with acknowledging who God is and establishing His reign and authority in our lives. We have got to say, "Lord, you reign and I surrender to your will." We have to make up our mind that we are going to follow His will and stand upon His word to help us do so. So, this week, declare your deliverance. Profess what you know God has ordained for you to do and be in Jesus's name. Find a scripture or daily profession that will speak to your deliverance and profess it all the time and especially when temptation comes. God is with you and will bring you through!

Lord, please deliver me from…

This, I profess in Jesus' name!

Daily Profession of the Word of God Transformed My Life This Week By…

There Is No Place like Home

There is nothing like when you go home for the holidays; the family, the food, the fellowship, the smells of the kitchen, the laughter, and the memories of good times. Homes are so important to people, to family, to faith, to love. And most people are overjoyed by their first home or dream of the day when they will own one. Even Jesus said in John 14:1-3, *"Let not your heart be troubled, believe in God, believe also in me. In my Father's house, there are many mansions: if it were not so, I would have told you. I go to prepare a place for you. And if I go and prepare a place for you, I will come again and receive you unto myself; that where I am there you maybe also."* So, home is definitely a safe place where you belong and feel loved; whether it is at your aunt's house, a friend's house, or your own home. Home is definitely where the heart is. In the same way, Paul said in 1 Corinthians 6:19, *"Know ye not that your body is the temple of the Holy Ghost which is in you, which ye have of God, and ye are not your own?"*

In other words, our body is a home of the Holy Spirit, and we need to make sure we take care of it like we would our physical home or the people we love. Sometimes, our homes or our relationships can become dilapidated from the wind, rain, and storms of life. However, we must take care of what God established in us by spending time in His word, following His will, using His wisdom, and watching who we hang around and entertain. We must keep our temples pure by asking for forgiveness and showing God's love. There is no place like home. Therefore, our ultimate goal should be to reside with Jesus in heaven and be a light to those who do not know Him so they will want to live with Him, and He in them forever! This I profess in Jesus's name.

Daily Profess God's Word for "*There Is No Place like Home*"

> Let not your heart be troubled, believe in God, believe also in me. In my Father's house, there are many mansions: if it were not so, I would have told you. I go to prepare a place for you. And if I go and prepare a place for you, I will come again and receive you unto myself; that where I am there you maybe also. (Jn 14:1-3)
>
> What? Know ye not that your body is the temple of the Holy Ghost which is in you, which ye have of God, and ye are not your own. (1 Cor. 6:19)

For ye are bought with a price: therefore, glorify God in your body, and in your spirit, which are God's. (1 Cor. 6:20)

Except the LORD build the house, they labour in vain that build it: except the LORD keep the city, the watchman waketh but in vain. (Ps. 127:1)

The house of the wicked will be overthrown, but the tent of the upright will flourish. (Prov. 14:11)

In the house of the righteous there is much treasure, but in the revenue of the wicked is trouble. (Prov. 15:6)

Through wisdom a house is built, and by understanding it is established; by knowledge the rooms are filled with all precious and pleasant riches. (Prov. 24:3-4)

Which scripture speaks to you the most and why?

____

____

____

____

____

A Daily Challenge for You

Clean your home! This week, I challenge you to mentally and spiritually clean your temple. Take the time to get rid of any mental clutter of negative thoughts, bad experiences, grudges, unsettled relationships, or your own wrongdoings and lay them at your Father's feet in prayer. Pray about it, ask for forgiveness, pray for those who may have hurt you, or even talk to someone of godly counsel who can help you sort things out. Let this week be a stepping-stone to wipe out the old and fill your temple with the new; the joy, peace, and wisdom that God has already given to you. Then you can live your life free from bondage or sin, and focus more on what you can do for Jesus while here on earth.

I will cleanse my home (the temple of the Holy Spirit) by…

This, I profess in Jesus' name!

Daily Profession of the Word of God Transformed My Life This Week By…

There Is Nothing like the Presence of God!

There is nothing like the presence of God! In His presence, pain will leave, your mind will be calmed, your heart will be comforted, and your past will disappear. It is a place that you cannot describe but literally feel like you are floating in thin air with not a weight in the world to carry. When you really surrender to the presence of God and allow Him to take over your heart, your mind, and your soul, there is nothing you can't overcome. Everything you have been carrying begins to fade away. And it is because you realize His power. Psalm 97:5 says, "*The hills melted like wax at the presence of the Lord, at the presence of the Lord of the whole earth.*" So, even the elements that He created are subjected to His authority. There is nothing that He created that supersedes Him, not even the devil and any hell that has come your way.

So, walk in His presence, talk in His presence, and when you feel like you have gone astray, *run* to His presence. He is always with you and will never leave but you have to *surrender* your will to His. You have to lay on your face, bow down, and say your will not mine Lord! Do it in me! Crucify my flesh! Help me to experience the Savior that you are and rest in the grace of your unconditional love. It is in His presence that there is fullness of joy (Psalm 16:11). So, stay there. Stay in His presence, stay in His Word and worship Him daily. He will give you everything you need, the peace of mind you so desire, the deliverance you are praying for, and even *more...*

Daily Profess God's Word for *"There Is Nothing like the Presence of God"*

> The hills melted like wax at the presence of the Lord, at the presence of the Lord of the whole earth. (Ps. 97:5)
>
> Thou wilt shew me the path of life: in thy presence is fullness of joy; at thy right hand there are pleasures for evermore. (Ps. 16:11)
>
> And he said, My presence shall go [with thee], and I will give thee rest. (Exod. 33:14)
>
> When thou saidst, Seek ye my face; my heart said unto thee, Thy face, Lord, will I seek. (Ps. 27:8)
>
> Blessed are the pure in heart: for they shall see God. (Matt. 5:8)

> But the Comforter, [which is] the Holy Ghost, whom the Father will send in my name, he shall teach you all things, and bring all things to your remembrance, whatsoever I have said unto you. (Jn 14:26)

> And ye shall seek me, and find me, when ye shall search for me with all your heart. (Jer. 29:13)

> God is a Spirit: and they that worship him must worship him in spirit and in truth. (Jn 4:24)

Which scripture speaks to you the most and why?

____

____

____

____

____

A Daily Challenge for You

One thing you have to remember is that God is always waiting on you to enter into the fullness of His presence. Yes, He will never leave you or forsake you (Heb. 13:5). However, if you sit still long enough and truly seek His face, you will experience the presence of God like never before. You will hear His voice speak to you through His word and feel the comfort of His warm embrace. Just take the time this week to not just pray and talk to God about everything, but make sure to rest in His presence, worship Him, and let Him give you peace and the overflow of His love.

I will rest in the presence of God by…

____

____

____

____

____

____

____

____

____

____

____

This, I profess in Jesus' name!

Daily Profession of the Word of God Transformed My Life This Week By...

Use Your Spiritual Weapons

As you go higher in your walk with God, the attack of the enemy will increase. Satan will try to throw you off-track with unforeseen circumstances, trials at work, family issues, mistakes you make, or even faults of your own. However, the Bible is clear in 2 Cor. 10:3-5, *"For though we walk in the flesh, we do not war according to the flesh: (For the weapons of our warfare are not carnal, but mighty through God to the pulling down of strongholds), casting down arguments, and every high thing that exalts itself against the knowledge of God, and bringing into captivity every thought to the obedience of Christ."*

God has given us the tools to defeat whatever the enemy may send through prayer, fasting, and by reading His word. These are the weapons of warfare that He has given us to pull down strongholds like lying, deception, gossip, guilty pleasures, ties that bind in relationships, and even a negative mind-set, or a double-minded way of thinking. He has given us the authority to cast down every high thing of the world that would try and convince you to operate against the knowledge that God has given you to live a life of freedom with joy and peace, victoriously, for Him! We just have to use it. We need to ask God to increase our discernment and give us the wisdom we need to follow Him, even when the enemy tries to get us to lose our focus in things going wrong. As long as we stay humble before God and use the weapon of His Word, which is the Sword of the Spirit, He will fight the battle with His angelic hosts and deliver us from the bondage we are in!

Daily Profess God's Word and *Use Your Spiritual Weapons*

For though we walk in the flesh, we do not war according to the flesh: (For the weapons of our warfare are not carnal, but mighty through God to the pulling down of strongholds), casting down arguments, and every high thing that exalts itself against the knowledge of God, and bringing into captivity every thought to the obedience of Christ. (2 Cor. 10:3-5)

Have I not commanded you? Be strong and of a good courage; be not afraid, neither be thou dismayed: for the Lord your God is with you wherever you go. (Josh. 1:9)

The Lord is on my side; I will not fear: what can man do unto me? (Ps. 118:6)

What shall we then say to these things? If God is for us, who can be against us? (Rom. 8:31)

As it is written, For your sake we are killed all the day long; we are accounted as sheep for the slaughter. Nay, in all these things we are more than conquerors through Him that loved us. (Rom. 8:36-37)

Fear not; for I am with you: be not dismayed; for I am your God: I will strengthen you; yea, I will help you; yea, I will uphold you with the right hand of my righteousness. (Is. 41:10)

I sought the LORD, and He heard me, and delivered me from all my fears. (Ps. 34:4)

Humble yourselves therefore under the mighty hand of God, that He may exalt you in due time: Casting all your care upon Him; for He cares for you. (1 Pet. 5:6-7)

Peace I leave with you; my peace I give unto you: not as the world gives, give I unto you. Let not your heart be troubled, neither let it be afraid. (Jn 14:27)

The LORD shall fight for you, and you shall hold your peace. (Exod. 14:14)

Which scripture speaks to you the most and why?

____

____

____

____

____

A Daily Challenge for You

It is so easy to succumb to fear or to get distracted by what bad is going on. Your body, your mind, and your soul naturally wants to give your attention to it and will become overwhelmed by it. However, you have to remember that Satan would not be coming nigh you unless you were doing something powerful for God's Kingdom. Ultimately, he wants to get you off-track so that other people cannot experience God's deliverance through your life. So when the distractions, trials, or issues arise, *immediately* give them to God and use your weapon of prayer, fasting, or profession of God's word. Lay it all at His feet and find a scripture that you can declare against it. God will keep you in perfect peace if you keep your mind stayed on Him (Isaiah 26:3).

When Satan tries to attack, I will use the weapon of ________________ by...

____

____

____

____

____

____

____

____

____

____

____

____

____

____

____

This, I profess in Jesus' name!

Daily Profession of the Word of God Transformed My Life This Week By...

We Are Covered and Protected!

In this day and time, we have got to *rejoice and be glad* about to whom we belong and who we are *covered* by! There are so many different things that keep happening in our world that can cause fear, doubt, or even tempt us to live in anxiety as to what will happen next. However, we have to declare that we are *covered and protected* in Jesus's name! When Jesus died on the cross for us, He shed His blood for the remission of our sins but He also gave us *victory* over death or anything that would come against us. So, there is no sin, no past bondage, no devil in hell, nor anything present that can separate us from the love of Jesus Christ (Romans 8:38-39). We have to declare and say "We are covered in Jesus's name!" If we can confess with our mouths and believe in our hearts that Jesus died and rose again just for us (Romans 10:9), then we can best believe that His protection over us as His children is not going to be any less when God made sure to *save* us!

We are covered by the blood of the Lamb! This is why *"perfect love casts out fear"* as it says in 1 John 4:18. Even when Jesus was born, attacks tried to come against Him, and fear tried to enter in His family when King Herod wanted to kill Him. However, God wanted to make it known that nothing can stop the light and love that I am sending into this dark world and even in death, Jesus still won because He rose again! When we fully understand that the same Jesus who died on the cross for us has also given us *victory* over death or any attack of the enemy, we can rejoice and be glad! Romans 8:37 says, *"We are more than conquerors through Him who loved us."* So, we must walk in that truth for Jesus said "I am the way, the truth, and the life. No one comes to the Father but by me." (Jn 14:6)

As long as we are under His care, we are *covered* and *protected* by the Father, and we do not have to fear what man or anyone else can do to our families, our cities, or our nations, because ultimately we have *everlasting life* with Him! So, let us rejoice and be glad in the truth that He was sent to *save* us and we have the victory through Jesus Christ our Lord! For we are in His hands and no one can pluck us out (John 10:28). This I profess in Jesus's name!

Daily Profess God's Word for "*We Are Covered and Protected*"

Nay, in all these things we are more than conquerors through him that loved us. (Rom. 8:37)

For I am persuaded, that neither death, nor life, nor angels, nor principalities, nor powers, nor things present, nor things to come, nor height, nor depth, nor any other creature, shall be able to separate us from the love of God, which is in Christ Jesus our Lord. (Rom. 8:38-39)

That if you shall confess with your mouth the Lord Jesus, and shall believe in your heart that God has raised him from the dead, you shall be saved. (Rom. 10:9)

Jesus saith unto him, I am the way, the truth, and the life: no man cometh unto the Father, but by me. (Jn 14:6)

There is no fear in love; but perfect love casts out fear, because fear involves torment. But he who fears has not been made perfect in love. (1 Jn 4:18)

And I give unto them eternal life; and they shall never perish, neither shall any man pluck them out of my hand. (Jn 10:28)

For this is my blood of the new testament, which is shed for many for the remission of sins. (Matt. 26:28)

Which scripture speaks to you the most and why?

____

____

____

____

____

____

____

____

____

____

A Daily Challenge for You

This week, your challenge is to declare the blood covering and protection of your family, your city, and our nation! Begin to profess His word on how He watches over you and rebuke any fears that come to mind or that may present itself to you this week. Then *rejoice* in the fact that you are firmly and securely in God's hands and watch Him show you His loved that saves you!

This week, I saw how God covers and protects us when He…

This, I profess in Jesus' name!

Daily Profession of the Word of God Transformed My Life This Week By…

What Do You Hear?

What do you hear God saying to you? Is He speaking what you want to hear, or is He saying something you don't want to hear? Is He telling you to show love to someone who you don't necessarily like, or is He telling you to spend more time with Him when you get up in the mornings? Either way, you have to ask yourself, "Am I ready and willing to respond to His call when I hear His voice? Whether He is calling me to fast for three days or give good news, will I respond quickly with obedience?"

This is the reality for believers because we know what God is saying. We hear it in our hearts, but sometimes, we hesitate or just flat out disobey Him. However, in the Bible, the prophet Samuel told King Saul in 1 Samuel 15:23, *"For rebellion is as the sin of witchcraft, and stubbornness is as iniquity and idolatry. Because you have rejected the word of the Lord, he has also rejected you from being king."* God wants us to respond to His call without question, and He wants us to obey the call on our lives. This is why the next time you hear God speak, move on it, for the blessing is on the other side of your obedience, and it will stop you from aborting your purpose. This I profess in Jesus's name!

Daily Profess God's Word for "*What Do You Hear?*"

For rebellion is as the sin of witchcraft, and stubbornness is as iniquity and idolatry. Because you have rejected the word of the Lord, he has also rejected you from being king. (1 Sam. 15:23)

My sheep hear my voice, and I know them, and they follow me. (Jn 10:27)

So then faith cometh by hearing, and hearing by the word of God. (Rom. 10:17)

He that is of God hears, God's words; ye therefore hear them not, because ye are not of God. (Jn 8:47)

And thine ears shall hear a word behind thee, saying, This is the way, walk ye in it, when ye turn to the right hand, and when ye turn to the left. (Is. 30:21)

But He said, Yea rather blessed are they that hear the word of God, and keep it. (Lk 11:28)

It is the spirit that gives life; the flesh profits nothing: the words that I speak unto you, they are spirit, and they are life. (Jn 6:63)

> I can of mine own self do nothing: as I hear, I judge: and my judgment is just; because I seek not mine own will, but the will of the Father which hath sent me. (Jn 5:30)

Which scripture speaks to you the most and why?

____

____

____

____

____

A Daily Challenge for You

Every day, God wants to speak to us. However, we all have to admit that a lot of times, we hear everybody else and even our voice above God's. For our mental and spiritual health, we have to clear our head, set aside everything else, and just spend time with God. Let's not make a list of what we need from God this week. Let's just hear His voice; hear what He has to say. Let Him guide you, lead you, and give you the wisdom to live out the call on your life. So, this week, write down what He says but also write down how you respond.

Lord, you are telling me to...

This, I profess in Jesus' name!

Daily Profession of the Word of God Transformed My Life This Week By...

What God Thinks of Me

God's thoughts of you are vast! They outweigh what anyone else thinks of you or what anyone else says. He loves you with a love that is everlasting and has intricately designed you for a marvelous purpose. Because He created you and never stops thinking about you, know that the highest level of servitude is to give everything to Him. All of you for all of Him is a "no brainer." There is nothing you could do to repay Him, nothing you could do to give Him *all* the honor and the glory that He is due. You just have to serve Him with your whole heart. Give Him every part of you; your mind, your body, and your soul. You have to die to yourself daily and let Him cultivate your life and lead you. For David said in Psalm 139:17-18 says, *"How precious also are thy thoughts unto me, O God! How great is the sum of them! If I should count them, they are more in number than the sand: when I awake, I am still with thee."*

God loves you unconditionally. And there is not a day or a moment that goes by that God does not think of you! So He knows the plans that He has for you. He knows how everything is going to work out and, most of all, He has already thought through how to get you to your destiny while enjoying the life He gave you as a child of the king.

So, rest your mind and know that what God thinks of you is all you need!

Daily Profess God's Word for *"What God Thinks of Me"*

Your eyes did see my substance, being yet unformed; and in your book they were all written, the days fashioned for me, when as yet there were none of them. (Ps. 139:16)

How precious also are thy thoughts unto me, O God! How great is the sum of them! (Ps. 139:17)

If I should count them, they are more in number than the sand: when I awake, I am still with thee. (Ps. 139:18)

What is man, that you are mindful of him? and the son of man, that you visit him? (Ps. 8:4)

For my thoughts are not your thoughts, neither are your ways my ways, saith the Lord. (Is. 55:8)

For as the heavens are higher than the earth, so are my ways higher than your ways, and my thoughts than your thoughts. (Is. 55:9)

O Lord, how great are your works! And your thoughts are very deep. (Ps. 92:5)

For who has known the mind of the Lord, that He may instruct him? But we have the mind of Christ. (1 Cor. 2:16)

Many, O Lord my God, are your wonderful works which you have done, and your thoughts which are toward us: they cannot be recounted in order unto you: If I would declare and speak of them, they are more than can be numbered. (Ps. 40:5)

Lord, what is man, that you take knowledge of him! Or the son of man, that you make account of him! (Ps. 144:3)

Which scripture speaks to you the most and why?

____

____

____

____

____

____

A Daily Challenge for You

I cannot help but wonder what we did to deserve this type of love! The fact that God loves us the way He does and thinks of us more than the number of grains of sand is mind-blowing. Our God! Our glorious God! God deserves every part of us, and you can live your life every day knowing that He is thinking of you. Therefore, everything is going to be just fine. All you have to do is spend time with Him in His Word, hear His thoughts, and enjoy your life knowing that God thinks the world of you!

God thinks I am…

____

____

____

____

____

____

____

____

This I profess in Jesus' name!

Daily Profession of the Word of God Transformed My Life This Week By…

Why Did This Happen?

In the midst of the tragedy of the death of Walter Scott Sr. in North Charleston, SC, we found ourselves asking, Why? Why did Walter run? Why did the officer shoot him down and murder him? Why are such injustices all across our country? Why do we live in a world, in a country, in a city where our lives can be sometimes gripped with fear because we do not know what man is going to do?

Questions like these can put us in a tailspin and cause us to be uncertain about life, even when we go through our own personal situations and ask why did this happen. However, when I sat down the other day and asked God for wisdom and to just give me peace in the midst of praying for the Scott family, our country, and so many others, He said, "Just ask in my name and I will give it to you." Proverbs 18:10 says, *"The name of the Lord is a strong tower; the righteous runs into it, and is safe."* Therefore, we have a place to rest! We have the name of our Lord and Savior Jesus Christ that we can trust in and all we have to do is ask for peace and wisdom Jesus name and He will do it (John 14:13). We do not have to be overwhelmed or consumed! For even David said to the Philistine in 1 Samuel 17:45, *"You come to me with a sword, and with a spear, and with shield: but I come to you in the name of the Lord of hosts, the God of the armies of Israel, whom you have defied."* God is the One we can rest in forever! He will give us the peace and the direction we need to be used by Him so that we can help bring healing, hope, and reconciliation to a nation that needs Him.

Daily Profess God's Word for "*Why Did This Happen?*"

In my distress I cried to the Lord, and He heard me. (Ps. 120:1)

The name of the Lord is a strong tower; the righteous runs into it, and is safe. (Prov. 18:10)

You come to me with a sword, and with a spear, and with shield: but I come to you in the name of the Lord of hosts, the God of the armies of Israel, whom you have defied. (1 Sam. 17:45)

And whatsoever ye shall ask in my name, that will I do, that the Father may be glorified in the Son. (Jn 14:13)

And not only *that,* but we also glory in tribulations, knowing that tribulation produces perseverance;

and perseverance, character; and character, hope. Now hope does not disappoint, because the love of God has been poured out in our hearts by the Holy Spirit who was given to us. (Rom. 5:3-5)

God has not given us a spirit of fear, but of power, love, and a sound of mind. (2 Tim. 1:7)

Fear not, for I *am* with you; be not dismayed, for I *am* your God. I will strengthen you, yes, I will help you, I will uphold you with My righteous right hand. (Is. 41:10)

Which scripture speaks to you the most and why?

____

____

____

____

____

____

____

____

A Daily Challenge for You

There is no answer to justify evil or the reasons why someone carries it out. And it is hard sometimes to understand why bad things happen. However, God is still in control. We live in a world where people can choose evil, but we can choose to trust God even in the midst of it. We can choose to believe in Him, rest in Him, and know that He is our protector. For this earth is not our final destination, but living in Heaven with Him is our eternal home. So, walk by faith and not by sight. Lean and depend upon God every day. He is the only one who keeps us safe forever!

I choose to trust God and rest in the fact that He will…

This, I profess in Jesus' name!

Daily Profession of the Word of God transformed my life this week by...

Why Trust God?

We always look to man to fulfill our needs. You can say you don't, but as human beings, we do. It is natural for us to look to someone who is physically right there in front of us to provide our every need, whether it is material, emotional, and even spiritual. We sometimes even depend on the preacher to give us a word when God can speak through them and us too. We have to put our *trust* in God, not man. Psalm 118:8 says, *"It is better to trust in the Lord than to put confidence in man."* In other words, the writer, David, realized that man is unstable, man can change his feelings from one day to the next, and man can let you down. However, God is faithful. God is the same yesterday, today, and forevermore (Hebrews 13:8). God will never leave you nor forsake you (Hebrews 13:5). God knows more about you than you know about yourself (Psalm 139:3-4). God sees beyond what you see. And *"God is not a man, that He should lie"* (Num. 23:19). God knows what is best for you! There is not a situation or an issue that God cannot handle or supersede. So, it is better to put your trust in God than man, because God is eternal and will never end. He is the one that we should lean upon, depend upon, and trust His word over what any other man says or thinks. He is the one who is a constant friend!

Daily Profess God's Word for *"Why Trust God?"*

It is better to trust in the Lord than to put confidence in man. (Ps. 118:8)

God is not a man, that He should lie; neither the son of man, that He should repent: has He said, and shall He not do it? Or has He spoken, and shall He not make it good? (Num. 23:19)

You search out my path and my lying down, and are acquainted with all my ways. For there is not a word in my tongue, but, lo, O Lord, you know it altogether. (Ps. 139:3-4)

And now, O Lord God, you are that God, and your words are true, and you have promised this goodness unto your servant. (2 Sam. 7:28)

And they that know your name will put their trust in you, for you, Lord, have not forsaken them that seek you. (Ps. 9:10)

Some trust in chariots and some in horses, but we trust in the name of the LORD our God. (Ps. 20:7)

But I trust in your unfailing love; my heart rejoices in your salvation. (Ps. 13:5)

O LORD Almighty, blessed is the man who trusts in you. (Ps. 84:12)

But I trust in you, O LORD; I say, "You are my God." (Ps. 31:14)

Which scripture speaks to you the most and why?

____

____

____

____

____

A Daily Challenge for You

At the end of the day, there is always going to be the temptation to put your trust in man or even in yourself. However, the Bible is clear in Proverbs 28:26 when it says, *"He who trusts in himself is a fool, but he who walks in wisdom is kept safe."* You have got to remember that God has already made His reputation. He said, "For I am the LORD, I change not." (Mal. 3:6). He knows your end and your beginning. So, trust in Him, and Him alone who created you!

I will trust God because...

____

____

____

____

____

____

____

____

____

____

____

____

This, I profess in Jesus' name!

Daily Profession of the Word of God Transformed My Life This Week By…

You Will *Grow* Through it in Jesus' Name!

I have been so blessed to witness the testimonies of so many who have gone through trials, tribulations, even thoughts of suicide, and God still brought them out because they stayed in the house of God! I witnessed people firsthand share how they cried out to God in their distress, and He heard them and delivered them. These stories were shared because they realized that it was their faith and trust in God and even their commitment to still go to church and worship that caused them to *grow* through it and out of it. It was because of His grace and mercy and the love of the Father that enabled them to see themselves beyond their situation and *hope* for more!

I realized, now more than ever, that we are all real people with real issues serving a *real God*! We can act like everything is okay all the time, but the reality is that if it had not been for Jesus on our side, where would we be? We need to share our testimonies and let people see how good He is. We need to witness to others about our salvation and how good it is to be in a personal relationship with Christ. We need to be around other believers who serve God and who can encourage us. Most importantly, we need to remember God blesses us when we stay in the house of the Lord! That is true *growth*; when we don't mind sharing how God has brought us up and out for the world to see so that people may come to know Him. All in all, Psalm 92:12-13 says it best, that *"The righteous shall flourish like the palm tree: he shall grow like a cedar in Lebanon. Those that be planted in the house of the Lord shall flourish in the courts of our God."* So, be encouraged today to know, that despite what you go through, if you stay faithful and dwell in the house of the Lord, you will *grow* through it and flourish in Jesus's name!

Daily Profess God's Word and *You Will Grow Through It in Jesus' Name!*

> The righteous shall flourish like the palm tree: he shall grow like a cedar in Lebanon. Those that be planted in the house of the Lord shall flourish in the courts of our God. (Ps. 92:12-13)
>
> But grow in grace, and in the knowledge of our Lord and Savior Jesus Christ. To him be glory both now and forever. Amen. (2 Pet. 3:18)
>
> I have planted, Apollos watered; but God gave the increase. So then neither is he that plants any-

thing, neither he that waters; but God that gives the increase. (1 Cor. 3:6-7)

He that trusts in his riches shall fall: but the righteous shall flourish as a branch. (Prov. 11:28)

They shall still bring forth fruit in old age; they shall be healthy and flourishing. (Ps. 92:14)

In whom all the building fitly framed together grows unto a holy temple in the Lord: In whom you also are built together for a habitation of God through the Spirit. (Eph. 2:21-22)

Not boasting of things beyond our measure, that is, of other men's labors; but having hope, when your faith is increased, that we shall be strengthened by you according to our field abundantly. (2 Cor. 10:15)

In his days shall the righteous flourish; and abundance of peace so long as the moon endures. (Ps. 72:7)

Which scripture speaks to you the most and why?

____

____

____

____

____

A Daily Challenge for You

It really does not matter what you are going through and how much you have had to endure. With God, nothing is impossible and He can see you through it. However, you have to make sure you put yourself in the right position to receive the blessings He has for you. You have to stay in His presence, read His word, fellowship with other saints who can help strengthen your faith. If you have not found a church home, or a ministry to serve in, make it a point this week to start looking for where God wants you to be so that you can *grow*. If you have already found a place of worship, then make sure to share your testimonies with someone else, and commit to serving in that area. You never know, what you do and what you share may help them *grow* through it in Jesus name.

I will grow through it by…

This, I profess in Jesus' name!

Daily Profession of the Word of God Transformed My Life This Week By…

Your Set Time of Favor Is Here!

As I sit back and reflect, one powerful week comes to mind when we had our Bishop's Conference at The Revelation of Christ Church in Charleston, South Carolina where Pastor Lance T. Johnson Sr., my husband, is our pastor. We felt His glory in ways like we have never known and heard revelation through His word like never before. And it was then that I realized that when you truly want to hear from God and *expect* God to speak to you and catapult you to the next level in your destiny, He will do it! One of the bishops shared the scripture of Psalm 102:13 which says, *"You shall arise, and have mercy upon Zion: for the time to favor her, yes, the set time, is come."* He spoke of how this is the time to walk through the "open door" in your walk with Christ, in your career, in your ministry, that God has mercifully granted to you, so that you can fulfill God's plan for your life and reach more souls for Christ. So, I ask you today to seek God like you never have before! Take the challenge of walking through that "open door" in your relationship with God, to hear His voice through His word, so you can receive the direction you need to fulfill your destiny. There is something God has placed on the inside of you that, as a believer, is stirring within you to be used for His kingdom. So whatever gifts and talents He has blessed you with, use them for the Lord! Trust Him and be obedient to what He has called you to do. He will advance you for *your set time of favor is here*!

Daily Profess God's Word for *Your Set Time of Favor Is Here*

You shall arise, and have mercy upon Zion: for the time to favor her, yes, the set time, is come. (Ps. 102:13)

For thou, Lord, wilt bless the righteous; with favor wilt thou compass him as with a shield. (Ps. 5:12)

For the Lord God is a sun and shield: the Lord will give grace and glory: no good thing will he withhold from them that walk uprightly. (Ps. 84:11)

In whom also we have obtained an inheritance, being predestinated according to the purpose of him who worketh all things after the counsel of his own will. (Eph. 1:11)

For his anger endureth but a moment; in his favour is life: weeping may endure for a night, but joy cometh in the morning. (Ps. 30:5)

> And said, My Lord, if now I have found favour in thy sight, pass not away, I pray thee, from thy servant. (Gen. 18:3)

> And the Lord shall guide thee continually, and satisfy thy soul in drought, and make fat thy bones: and thou shalt be like a watered garden, and like a spring of water, whose waters fail not. (Is. 58:11)

> And Jesus increased in wisdom and stature, and in favour with God and man. (Lk 2:52)

Which scripture speaks to you the most and why?

____

____

____

____

____

A Daily Challenge for You

There are many doors that are open to you every day and many choices you can make. It is your responsibility to sit still before God long enough to hear which one He has predestined you to go through. In other words, you have to ask God, What door have you opened for me? What steps can I take that reflect the favor that God has placed upon my life? Spend time with God and let him show you the way of favor that He wants you to take so that He alone can get the glory and you can fulfill your destiny!

Lord, I will walk through your open door of favor by…

____

____

____

____

____

____

____

____

____

____

____

This, I profess in Jesus' name!

Daily Profession of the Word of God Transformed My Life This Week By…

Your Ultimate Purpose

People spend a lot of time, money, and effort in trying to figure out what their purpose is in life. They go to seminars, conferences, attend college, postgraduate study, and even put children in camps just so they can find their purpose. Everyone wants to find out why they were put on this earth and what they have been called to do. However, our ultimate purpose for being here on this earth is to glorify God and to help save more souls for Christ! No matter what we do or what profession we are in, God created us to bring Him glory. He wants to show His power through our lives, so whatever gifts and talents He has given us were ultimately endowed in us to help touch someone else's life and reach more souls for Him. Revelation 4:11 says, *"You are worthy, O Lord, to receive glory and honor and power: for you have created all things, and for your pleasure they are and were created."* Knowing this, God is not going to call us to do anything that does not lift up His name. We can look at what we are blessed with the ability to do and use it to give glory and honor to Him so that people will desire to have a relationship with Jesus Christ and live out their God-given purpose too!

Daily Profess God's Word for *Your Ultimate Purpose*

You are worthy, O Lord, to receive glory and honor and power: for you have created all things, and for your pleasure they are and were created. (Rev. 4:11)

For it is God who works in you both to will and to do of His good pleasure. (Phil. 2:13)

Let your light so shine before men that they may see your good works and glorify your Father who is in the heavens. (Matt. 5:16)

As obedient children, not fashioning yourselves according to the former lusts in your ignorance: But as He who has called you is holy, so be holy in all manner of conduct. (1 Pet. 1:14-15)

But we all, with unveiled face beholding as in a mirror the glory of the Lord, are changed into the same image from glory to glory, even as by the Spirit of the Lord. (2 Cor. 3:18)

Whether therefore you eat, or drink, or whatsoever you do, do all to the glory of God. (1 Cor. 10:31)

What? Know you not that your body is the temple of the Holy Ghost which is in you, which you have of God, and you are not your own? For you are bought with a price: therefore glorify God in your body, and in your spirit, which are God's. (1 Cor. 6:19-20)

For we are His workmanship, created in Christ Jesus unto good works, which God had before ordained that we should walk in them. (Eph. 2:10)

And whatsoever you do, do it heartily, as to the Lord, and not unto men; knowing that of the Lord you shall receive the reward of the inheritance: for you serve the Lord Christ. (Col. 3:23-24)

Which scripture speaks to you the most and why?

____

____

____

____

____

____

____

A Daily Challenge for You

It is time to live out your ultimate purpose, which is to glorify God in all that you do! You do not have to worry or fret anymore about what God has planned for you. All you have to do is seek to please Him every day by drawing closer to Him through His Word, and use what He has naturally given you to be a witness for Him in this world. He will then reveal to you what your destiny is and you will fulfill it!

My ultimate purpose is to glorify God by…

____

____

____

____

____

____

____

____

____

____

This, I profess in Jesus' name!

Daily Profession of the Word of God Transformed My Life This Week By...

Made in the USA
Columbia, SC
05 May 2018